Russia and NATO since 1991

Since the re-emergence of Russia as an independent state in December 1991, debates and controversies surrounding its evolving relations with NATO have been a prominent feature of the European security scene. This is the first detailed and comprehensive book-length analysis of Russia–NATO relations, covering the years 1991–2005. This new volume investigates the nature and substance of the 'partnership' relations that have developed between Russia and NATO during this time. It looks at the impact that the Kosovo crisis, September 11th, the Iraq war and the creation of the NATO–Russia Council have had on this complex relationship. The author concludes that Russia and NATO have, so far, developed a pragmatic partnership, but one that may potentially develop into a more significant strategic partnership.

This book will appeal to students and scholars of international relations, European politics and European security.

Martin A. Smith is Senior Lecturer in Defence and International Affairs at the Royal Military Academy, Sandhurst, UK. His main research interests are in international and European security, with a particular focus on post-Cold War NATO.

Routledge Advances in International Relations and Global Politics

Russia and NATO since 1991

From Cold War through cold peace to partnership?

Martin A. Smith

Routledge
Taylor & Francis Group

LONDON AND NEW YORK

First published 2006
by Routledge
2 Park Square, Milton Park, Abingdon, Oxon OX14 4RN

Simultaneously published in the USA and Canada
by Routledge
270 Madison Ave, New York, NY 10016

Transferred to Digital Printing 2007

Routledge is an imprint of the Taylor & Francis Group, an informa business

Typeset by RefineCatch Limited, Bungay, Suffolk
Printed and bound in Great Britain by
TJI Digital, Padstow, Cornwall

British Library Cataloguing in Publication Data
A catalogue record for this book is available from the British Library

Library of Congress Cataloging in Publication Data
Smith, Martin A., 1965–

Russia and NATO since 1991 : from cold war through cold peace to
partnership? / Martin A. Smith. – 1st ed.

p. cm. – (Routledge advances in international relations and global
politics)
Includes bibliographical references and index.

1. Security, International. 2. National security–Europe. 3. North
Atlantic Treaty Organization–Russia (Federation) I. Title. II. Series.
JZ6005.S65 2006
355′.031′0918210947–dc22

2005013139

ISBN10: 0–415–36300–4
ISBN13: 9–78–0–415–36300–6

Contents

Acknowledgements

Help and assistance above and beyond the call of duty was provided during the course of writing this book by my colleague David Brown and by Dmitry Polikanov. Both were kind enough to read and comment on drafts of the entire manuscript. In doing so, they saved me from several errors of fact, suggested new and better ways of interpreting and understanding the evidence and tidied up my grammar. I am particularly grateful to them both.

I would also like to thank Andrew Orgill and his team at the RMAS Library who were, as usual, unfailingly helpful in responding to my numerous requests for books and articles. The University of Bradford Library kindly issued me with a reader's ticket at the start of the research for this book, and subsequently renewed it. I was thus able to gain access to their invaluable holdings of English language translations of Russian source materials. The research here has benefited significantly as a result.

Finally, I wish to acknowledge the support of the team at Routledge/ Taylor and Francis: Craig Fowlie, Heidi Bagtazo, Grace McInnes and Harriet Brinton. I am especially grateful for their patience when an unexpected Sandhurst commitment temporarily held up final completion of this project.

Martin A. Smith
Camberley
April 2005

1 The Soviet Union, Russia and the 'Common European Home'

A foundation on which to build?

Introduction

In the years 1985–91, there was substantial debate and discussion in the Soviet Union, Western Europe and the United States on the prospects for the construction of a 'Common European Home'. This concept had been advanced as a key stated foreign policy goal by Mikhail Gorbachev, the last Soviet leader. Following the ending of the Cold War, more immediate and parochial security concerns moved centre-stage for much of the 1990s. They arose principally as a result of the conflicts attending the disintegration of the Yugoslav State and from the consequences of the break-up of the Soviet Union itself. The Common Home concept fell out of fashion, and during this decade, it was discussed relatively infrequently, if at all.

Nevertheless, from the perspective of the discussions in this volume, the Common Home concept forms a useful starting-point. The present author is interested in the nature of the post-Cold War security order in Europe and, in particular, the ways and the extent to which Russia – as the Soviet Union's principal successor – has been developing 'partnership' relations with one of the two core international institutions that constitute the contemporary 'West'.[1] In Cold War times, 'the West' was, of course, the main identified ideological and potential military adversary of the Soviet Union and its then allies in what was generally referred to as 'Eastern Europe'.[2]

In order to help us understand the origins and background to the ideas about partnership that have been generated since Russia re-emerged on the international stage in December 1991, this first chapter will begin by assessing the nature of the Common Home concept. It will then examine the reasons that prevented Gorbachev's vision from being realised in the late 1980s and conclude by asking what, if any, 'residue' was left behind, to potentially be picked up by Russian and western policy makers in the 1990s and beyond.

Gorbachev's concept

When assessing the Common European Home idea as advanced and developed by Gorbachev in the second half of the 1980s, three issues and questions are of particular importance in helping us to get to grips with it. They are, first, the anticipated place and role of the United States in the Common Home. Second, there was the projected role and place of the Soviet Union itself. Finally, what about the institutional 'architecture' of the prospective Common Home? The discussions that follow will examine these three core issues in turn.

The United States' place in the home

In his memoirs, first published in 1995, Gorbachev asserted that 'the idea of Europe as our Common Home had been a spontaneous thought' which first occurred to him on a visit to France (his first foreign trip as Soviet leader) in October 1985.[3] In reality, by that time, the term already had something of a pedigree in Cold War Soviet politics. It was at least implicit in the Soviet diplomatic manoeuvrings of 1953–4, which produced a proposal for what would, eventually, become the Conference on Security and Co-operation in Europe (CSCE), founded in Helsinki in 1975.[4] At the time that it was first made, this Soviet proposal had generated no interest amongst NATO states, mainly for the reason that it seemed to them that it was motivated primarily by a divisive agenda. That is to say, western leaders felt that the Soviets were attempting to drive a wedge between the United States and its NATO allies in Europe by creating a security system which either excluded the former altogether, or else confined it to the status of an invited guest and mere observer.[5] The Soviet Union, on the other hand, was portrayed in the proposal as being an integral part of 'Europe', and, hence, entitled to full participation rights in any pan-European arrangements, on account of its geography, culture and history.[6]

The NATO response to these Soviet ideas established a precedent for early western suspicion of proposals for pan-European security arrangements. The suspicion was founded on the belief that the Soviet Union remained consistently wedded to its divisive agenda. It was, as noted, to be over twenty years before the CSCE was eventually established. It was finally brought into being at the height of the Cold

War *détente* era, by which time western governments had come round to the view that engaging with the Soviets in a pan-European process might offer useful advantages. This was felt to be the case in two main areas. First, developing a military confidence-building regime could contribute to the stabilisation of the East–West stand-off and reduce the threat of large-scale aggression. Second, as part of the overall package, a human rights dimension was included at the insistence of both western governments and those of most of the so-called neutral and non-aligned states in Europe. This entailed the Soviet government, in common with virtually all other CSCE participants,[7] signing up to a set of norms prescribing 'civilised behaviour', with regard to respecting and protecting the human rights of its citizens. For their part, the Soviets had, in the meantime, helped to facilitate the creation of the pan-European forum by conceding the principle that the Americans would be *full* participants in it.

The then Soviet leader, Leonid Brezhnev, first explicitly used the phrase 'Europe is our Common Home' in a speech in November 1981. He did so against the backdrop of rising Cold War tensions. These were as a result of the Soviet invasion of Afghanistan, unrest in Poland and, especially, the recent decision by NATO member states to deploy intermediate-range nuclear missiles in Western Europe from autumn 1983. Given this backdrop, Brezhnev's appeal to a shared European destiny was not likely to sway many minds amongst western governments. Scepticism was reinforced by the fact that it seemed apparent from a reading of Brezhnev's remarks that he was pursuing a divisive approach, albeit a subtly couched one. The tenor of his speech was to portray the US and Europe in an 'us-and-them' context. He argued that the US was a foreign power, dedicated to increasing the risks of war in Europe by effectively forcing its new nuclear missiles on European countries. He contrasted his vision of a Common European Home with the American view, which, he alleged, saw Europe merely as a 'theater of military operations'.[8] Thus, although the US had formally been accepted as a full participant in the CSCE in the 1970s, it seemed apparent that the Soviet government remained committed to trying to exploit any differences and to driving wedges between the US and its allies in Europe.

In the months immediately following his accession to power in 1985, Gorbachev's speeches and other Soviet pronouncements pursued similar, traditional, themes. They were, thus, hardly likely to induce western states to significantly reassess Common Home ideas. A leading Sovietologist, Neil Malcolm, detected little difference between Gorbachev's early foreign policy statements and those of his predecessors on this issue. Nevertheless, Malcolm argued that debates were going on behind the scenes that promised some sort of revision of the long-standing Soviet divisive approach.[9] In his major public speech during the October 1985 visit to France, referred to earlier, Gorbachev had, at first sight, merely reiterated the traditional us-and-them view of the relationship between 'Europe' (including, in his reckoning, the Soviet Union) and the United States. Yet, on closer inspection, his remarks signalled a potentially significant concession in official Soviet thinking. He explicitly denied any divisive objectives and declared that 'we are realists, and we understand how strong the ties – historical, political, economic – are that link Western Europe with the US'.[10] This could be read as *de facto* acceptance on Gorbachev's part that, like it or not, any new or revamped Common Home would need to be based on a definitive Soviet acceptance of full *and permanent* American participation.

Yet, at no time during the rest of his tenure did Gorbachev fully and finally resolve the question of the place and role of the US in his envisaged Common Home. His subsequent public statements varied and he seemed in two minds on the subject, doubtless reflecting tensions and divisions of opinion within the wider Soviet establishment. In a keynote speech in Prague in April 1987, the Soviet leader contended that 'our concept of the "all-European home" by no means implies an intention to slam the doors shut on anyone'.[11] He repeated this formulation in his public apologia, *Perestroika: New Thinking for Our Country and the World*, which was published in Europe and the US in the summer of 1987. Here, however, Gorbachev muddied the waters significantly by reasserting elements of the traditional us-and-them worldview. He argued that the US was not only a non-European power, but that it was also one whose culture posed a 'serious threat' to that of Europe and Europeans. Indeed, Gorbachev's comments in this book suggested that, although economic necessity and high politics undoubtedly required a substantial US–Soviet *rapprochement* by the late 1980s, on a personal level he regarded American culture and values as being both alien and threatening. He wrote, for example, that 'one can only wonder that a deep, profoundly intelligent and inherently humane European culture is retreating to the background before the primitive revelry of violence and pornography and the flood of cheap feelings and low thoughts' [from across the Atlantic].[12]

Gorbachev's view of the United States, in *Perestroika*, as being an essentially alien and worrisome power and presence in Europe, was also reflected in his statement that 'we would not like to see anyone kick in the doors of the European home and take the head of the table at *somebody else's apartment*. But then, that is the concern of the owner of the apartment' [emphasis added].[13] These comments, made at the time of 'high perestroika', when significant East–West arms control and disarmament agreements were at last being negotiated, reflected a remarkable apparent reversion to 'old thinking'. The view that the US was alien, hostile and did not really deserve more than observer status in the European home would not have seemed out of place in a statement by any of his Cold War Soviet predecessors.

Gorbachev did, subsequently, shift ground once more on this question. In July 1989, he told the Parliamentary Assembly of the Council of Europe that 'the USSR and the United States constitute a natural part of the European international-political structure. And their participation in its evolution is not only justified, but is also historically determined. No other approach is acceptable, nor could another approach bring forth results.'[14] It was fairly obvious what Gorbachev's intention was here – to try to head off those who suggested that the Soviet Union was at least as alien a presence in Europe as the United States. In this revised formulation, Gorbachev was clearly linking the place of the United States to that of the Soviet Union and arguing that 'Europe' should not be conceived of in excessively narrow geographical, historical or cultural terms.

By the summer of 1989 it was becoming increasingly apparent to many informed observers that the established Soviet-imposed order in Eastern Europe was likely to face growing and significant challenges. Indeed, Gorbachev's Council of Europe address is best remembered for his acceptance of the view that it was no longer permissible for states to impose their own social, economic or political systems on others by coercive means. Probably, therefore, the Soviet leader realised that he would increasingly have to rely on persuasive argument if he wished to ensure that his state did not become progressively more isolated or marginalised from the European mainstream.

In summary: by the late 1980s, the Soviet agenda was decreasingly concerned with trying to exclude the United States or downgrade its role in Europe. Increasingly, the focus was on seeking to ensure the continued inclusion and involvement of the Soviet Union itself.

Thus, it can be doubted whether Mikhail Gorbachev sincerely believed that the US was 'a natural part' of Europe. Rather, this was most likely mainly a tactical formulation designed to head-off those who would challenge the Soviet Union's own place in a Common European Home. By 1989, the parlous state of the Soviet economy, and the failure of the perestroika reform programmes to arrest its decline, made the Soviet leader increasingly keen – some might say desperate – to win sympathy and financial support amongst western governments. Overall, Gorbachev never formed a settled view of the role of the US in the Common European Home, and also never demonstrated that he had finally abandoned all vestiges of traditional Soviet divisive thinking on this issue.

The Soviet Union's place in the home

In contrast to this, the stance taken by Gorbachev and his supporters on the place of the Soviet Union was unvarying and consistent. It was that history, culture and geography all demonstrated – indeed dictated – that the Soviet Union was fully a part of Europe and, hence, of a Common European Home. Gorbachev's public speeches were replete with rhetoric along these lines. In Prague in 1987, for example, he asserted that 'we attach paramount importance to the European direction of our foreign policy. Why is this? Above all, our peoples live on this continent; together with others, they are the legitimate heirs to the civilisation that arose here, and they are making an inalienable contribution to its development.'[15] This was a theme that he repeated consistently through his years in power.

Gorbachev's pitch for his state to be considered as an integral part of European civilisation and culture was closely bound up with his drive to de-ideologise Soviet foreign policy. In his memoirs he wrote that:

> Reflecting on the goals to set for our new foreign policy, I found it increasingly difficult to see the multicoloured patchwork of Europe's political map as I used to see it before. I was thinking about the common roots of this multiform and yet fundamentally indivisible European civilization, and perceived with growing awareness the artificiality of the political blocs and the archaic nature of the 'iron curtain'.[16]

Gorbachev was asserting that the ideological divide, which had formed the heart of the Cold War order in Europe, was, ultimately, less important than the underlying cultural and civilisation commonalties which formed the foundations for the construction of the Common European Home. The logical correlation of this, if he meant it, was that at some point the Soviet Union would have to decisively break with its past Cold War behaviour. In its various guises this behaviour had been premised on the view that ideological distinctions were paramount and, further, that any defections of states from the Soviet to the western camp could not be permitted. This logic had informed the

Soviet decisions to violently suppress dissident and alleged secessionist groups and movements in the German Democratic Republic (GDR) in 1953, Hungary in 1956 and Czechoslovakia in 1968.

Gorbachev's new logic arguably played the key role in precipitating the process that led to the collapse of communist regimes throughout Eastern Europe in the second half of 1989. During his Council of Europe speech, in what was seen as a clear signal that the Soviet Union would not intervene to maintain the Cold War status quo by force, Gorbachev had declared that:

> The fact that European states belong to different social systems is a reality. The recognition of this historical fact and respect for the sovereign right of every nation to freely choose a social system constitute the major prerequisites for a normal European process ... The social and political orders in particular countries have changed in the past and may change in the future. But this change is the exclusive affair of the people of that country and their choice. Any interference in domestic affairs and any attempts to restrict the sovereignty of states – friends, allies or any others – are inadmissible.[17]

This clear signal from the Soviet leader to the effect that the communist governments in Eastern Europe were on their own helped galvanise the reformers in those states that were already implementing change (that is, Hungary and Poland). It also gave a fillip to dissidents and protest movements in those that were not (the GDR, Czechoslovakia, Bulgaria and Romania).

By thus de-ideologising Soviet policy and showing a willingness to 'let Eastern Europe go', Gorbachev was seeking to create conditions for further reductions in Soviet military spending and increased economic and technological assistance from western governments. Yet, although this was the most pressing immediate need, the impulse for the Gorbachev changes went deeper. Alan Collins has argued that the downgrading of ideology represented a deliberate effort on the part of the Soviet leader to eliminate the so-called 'security dilemma' from relations between the Soviet Union and the West. According to Collins, Gorbachev consciously set out to challenge and overcome aspects of Soviet 'policy that [gave] rise to insecurity in others'.[18] This effort would, if successful, help facilitate reductions in defence spending and encourage western leaders to be better disposed towards the Soviet Union. Over and above that, it would also demonstrate, hopefully conclusively, that the Soviet Union was fit and entitled to be a full part of 'Europe' and the Common European Home.

Put another way, Gorbachev's Common Home concept contained a *normative* dimension. In his Council of Europe speech in July 1989, he said that 'we visualise a common European home as a law-governed community', adding that 'we, for our part, have begun moving in that direction'.[19] The Soviet Union was, therefore, entitled to a full place in the Common Home on the basis of its new-found willingness to inculcate and operationalise shared values and standards, with regard to democratic behaviour and respect for human rights, with the member states of NATO.

The home's architecture

How did Gorbachev envisage his concept being developed, in terms of supporting structures and institutions? The main institutional framework should, he argued, be provided by the existing Conference on Security and Co-operation in Europe, suitably enhanced and upgraded.[20] From the Soviet perspective, the CSCE, notwithstanding its hitherto irksome human rights dimension, already had one very large advantage over all other European security institutions. As the only geographically and politically pan-European framework developed during the Cold War years, it was also the only one in which the Soviet Union and its Warsaw Pact allies were included as full and equal participants alongside the United States and its NATO allies.

To briefly recap: the process that eventually yielded the CSCE had been started by Soviet proposals back in 1954. In order to see these brought to fruition, Soviet leaders had been required to concede US participation as a full member in the process. The returns, however, were by no means insignificant from the Soviet point of view. Two in particular were important. As part of the so-called 'Basket One' of CSCE, all thirty-five original participants pledged to regard existing borders in Europe as 'inviolable'. For the Soviet leadership at the time, this was tantamount to western acceptance of the legitimacy of the Soviet bloc. The CSCE's Basket Two, meanwhile, covered 'co-operation in the field of economics . . . science and technology' and Soviet leaders hoped that this would help improve their country's access to western technology and financial loans.[21]

The bases of Gorbachev's interest in using the CSCE as the institutional foundation for the Common European Home, on the other hand, were those dimensions that his predecessors in Moscow had largely tried to ignore or else actively denigrated. Most particularly these were contained in Basket Three, which focused on 'co-operation in humanitarian and other fields'. For Gorbachev, this element of the

CSCE process was a crucial part of his efforts to radically improve East–West relations and bind the Soviet Union into the 'law-governed community' about which he had spoken in 1989.

At a CSCE summit meeting held in Paris in November 1990, Gorbachev was clear on the role that he envisaged for the pan-European process in the post-Cold War world:

> Now the ideas proclaimed in Helsinki [at the CSCE's founding conference in 1975] are gaining a real foothold. We can talk about a legally defined European space in the spheres of security, human rights, the economy, ecology and information as something completely attainable. The similar ideas of a 'European home', a 'European confederation' and a 'peaceful European order' are being incorporated in a kind of political project. All of us will have to work on its implementation in the 1990s.[22]

In earnest of his intent, Gorbachev lobbied his partners to agree to hold an important CSCE 'conference on the human dimension' in Moscow during 1991 (although, in the event, this was not convened during what remained of the Soviet Union's life).

The fact that CSCE members subsequently refused to meet in Moscow during the final year of Gorbachev's time in power is indicative of the problems that beset his vision for it, and the Soviet Union's place within it, during 1991. In January of that year, an attempt by the Baltic States of Lithuania and Latvia to pre-emptively declare full independence from the Soviet Union was met with the use of force by the Soviet army, with resulting loss of life. Although Gorbachev denied that he had given the order to use force, the Soviet Union suffered the political consequence of an attempt being made to censure it through the CSCE, at the instigation of the members of the then European Community. This was, as one British newspaper put it at the time, 'deeply embarrassing to the country that fought so hard to convince Western Europe of its genuine respect for human rights'.[23]

More generally, the fallout from the Baltic crackdown helped to provoke deterioration in Soviet relations with the CSCE just a few months after Gorbachev's bold proclamation at the Paris summit. The Soviet government blocked the censure process and followed up by limiting attempts to bolster the CSCE's ability to call member states to account for alleged human rights abuses at a meeting in Berlin in June 1991. It insisted that the body's new mechanism for dealing with emergency situations must respect the principle of non-interference in states' internal affairs.[24]

Thus, Gorbachev's stated desire for the CSCE to become the frame-work structure for a law-governed community for its members was beginning to look a little threadbare in the months immediately prior to the Soviet collapse at the end of 1991. It has subsequently been suggested that the Soviet commitment to enhancing the CSCE was less deeply or consistently held and pursued than many contemporary observers had believed. Dov Lynch has argued that the CSCE only really occupied a central place on the Gorbachev agenda for about a year; from late 1989 to the end of 1990. According to Lynch, it seemed at that time that the pan-European framework might play an import-ant role in managing the process of German unification in a way con-ducive to Soviet interests. Once the German question was settled and that nation unified in October 1990, however, Soviet interest, in Lynch's words, 'lost impetus'.[25]

The legacy that Gorbachev bequeathed to the new Russian state, which came into being in December 1991, was, therefore, one of an essentially un-built Common European Home. The role of the United States, the world's only remaining superpower, had not been definitively settled whereas the role of the Soviet Union had been, but only really in the eyes of Gorbachev and his supporters. Many doubted the nature and extent of the Soviet Union's (and Russia's) European credentials.[26] Finally, efforts to bolster and develop the CSCE as the main element of the home's architecture had barely begun before the Soviet Union itself started to undermine them. This lent weight to subsequent arguments that the Soviet leadership had seen the pan-European forum as a tactical means to achieving wider ends, rather than as being of significant intrinsic value in its own right.

Russia and the Pan-European process since 1991

Russian policy towards the CSCE during the first months of the coun-try's independent existence seemed to most commentators and obser-vers to be positive. The main CSCE event during this period was a summit meeting in Helsinki in July 1992. The Russian position at this meeting was widely regarded, both inside and outside Russia, as being helpful and constructive.

Amongst the decisions taken at the Helsinki summit were ones to set up a mechanism for CSCE peacekeeping operations and to create the post of High Commissioner on National Minorities (HCNM). The Russian government, under President Boris Yeltsin, was supportive of both moves. Then Foreign Minister Andrei Kozyrev was especially enthusiastic in his public assessments of the role of the new HCNM.

Kozyrev saw this CSCE official acting to bring diplomatic pressure to bear on the governments of the Baltic States, especially Latvia and Estonia,[27] where Russian leaders were suspicious that the human and political rights of substantial populations of ethnic Russians and Russian speakers were being denied or violated.[28]

The Russian government also supported successive CSCE decisions, taken between March 1992 and February 1993, to deploy mediation missions to try to broker solutions to conflicts in Georgia, Moldova and with regard to the territory of Nagorno-Karabakh, disputed between Armenia and Azerbaijan. The last was subsequently slated as the prospective location for the first CSCE peacekeeping operation, if an acceptable political settlement could be reached (something that has not happened to date). The significance of Russian acquiescence lay in the extent to which these decisions appeared to rebut allegations that the Russian government did not regard other former Soviet states as being fully independent. According to this line of argument, the Russian government was determined to keep international organisations and institutions of all kinds out of the former Soviet area and would reserve to itself the right to conduct 'peacekeeping' and other military operations there.

In general, Russian leaders at this time were against 'foreign' institutions (notably NATO) operating in the former Soviet area, but more persuadable about prospective roles for the – relatively few – institutions in which Russia had a prominent status. At this time, the Russian government evidently regarded the CSCE as an important element of European security. The same was true with regard to the United Nations. Although Russian leaders, arguably, did not believe that they needed UN authorisation for 'peacekeeping' operations in the former Soviet area,[29] this was certainly embraced if it was granted. At the same time, Russia welcomed a UN decision to recognise the Russian-led Commonwealth of Independent States as a regional organisation capable of conducting its own peacekeeping and related missions.

The period from the end of 1991 to the late summer of 1993 has often been referred to as 'the honeymoon' in relations between Russia and the West. Even when this early honeymoon was in full swing, however, clouds were already visible on the horizon. At a CSCE ministerial meeting in December 1992, Foreign Minister Kozyrev startled his counterparts with a strident speech that apparently announced a new hard-line, anti-western stance by the Russian government. He subsequently explained that this statement was not, in fact, a reformulation of existing policy, but rather had been intended as a warning shot to demonstrate the likely foreign policy priorities of a potential alternative Russian government.[30] This bizarre episode suggested to some that Russia was not, in fact, taking the CSCE completely seriously and was continuing the Soviet approach of (mis)using its fora and mechanisms for the purposes of tactical manoeuvring. The then German Foreign Minister, Klaus Kinkel, was quoted as saying that 'an international forum is not the place for such behaviour'.[31]

Changes in actual Russian policy did become apparent during 1993 and, especially, 1994. Two issues were important in this context. As Andrei Zagorski has put it, in 1993–4, Russia 'completely reversed' its position on possible CSCE peacekeeping operations in the former Soviet area, moving from a position of broad support to increasingly vocal opposition.[32] This *volte-face* reflected a paradox. On the one hand, the Yeltsin government was increasingly asserting the right for Russia to act in the former Soviet area without sanction from *any* 'outsiders', whether or not they included Russia as a member state.[33] On the other, there were indications of Russian disenchantment that CSCE members as a whole had proved unwilling to follow up the 1992 Helsinki agreement on peacekeeping with some tangible action.

The main area of dispute, however, was over the future of NATO. As the discussions in Chapter 3 of this volume will show, there was a significant deterioration in relations between Russia and NATO during 1994. Russian policy became increasingly geared towards seeking to prevent NATO becoming an overly dominant presence on the European security scene. This, in turn, had knock-on effects on Russian policy and attitudes towards the CSCE.

The main Russian diplomatic tactic to try to effect its government's aims *vis-à-vis* NATO during 1994 was to forcefully advance proposals ostensibly designed to make the CSCE *primus inter pares* amongst European security institutions. There were two main elements to these proposals, which were put forward and reiterated at various times by Yeltsin and Kozyrev in the course of the year. The first was a suggestion that a United Nations-style 'security council' be created for the CSCE.[34] This would, as in the UN case, be made up of the leading powers amongst the CSCE's membership (including, naturally, Russia) and it would be empowered to take executive decisions on behalf of the member states as a whole. The second element focused on making the CSCE – *de jure* and *de facto* – the lead agency in European security affairs. Sometimes a 'hierarchical' organisational structure would be mentioned, whilst on other occasions the preferred term of reference was to the potential 'co-ordinating role' of the CSCE *vis-à-vis* NATO, the European Union and other international organisations and institutions.[35]

In Chapter 3 it will be argued that one of the reasons why Russia–NATO relations deteriorated from early 1994 was because of growing Russian suspicion of the motives behind the new NATO Partnership for Peace (PfP) programme. This had been announced at a NATO summit meeting in January 1994. In turn, one of the main motivations behind the formulation of the new Russian ideas on the CSCE's future was to put up an alternative to PfP; or 'document No. 2' as *Segodnya* called it at the time.[36]

The major dispute, however, was undoubtedly over the prospect of NATO membership enlargement. By the time of the CSCE summit in Budapest in December 1994, NATO enlargement was becoming the overriding issue in European security affairs for the Russian government. This was demonstrated by the extent to which President Yeltsin chose to make it the dominant theme of his keynote speech at the summit, during which he (in)famously warned western leaders of the risk of Europe 'plunging into a "cold peace" '.[37]

Some observers later argued that the near-obsession of Russian leaders in Budapest with the NATO enlargement issue meant that they missed, or were blind to, opportunities to strengthen the CSCE in practical ways.[38] For the record, neither of the two main Russian proposals for the CSCE's future, discussed above, was adopted at the summit. Indeed, about the only development was the change of name to Organization for Security and Co-operation in Europe (OSCE).

The OSCE in Chechnya

In December 1994, almost immediately following the Budapest summit, President Yeltsin ordered the Russian military to intervene in the rebellious Republic of Chechnya to try and stamp out an armed separatist movement there. The deteriorating security situation in Chechnya may well have contributed to the general testiness and defensiveness of the Russian leadership at the CSCE/OSCE summit. More positively, in April 1995, agreement was reached to dispatch an OSCE Assistance Group to Chechnya (AG), in order to help with humanitarian relief and with the search for a political settlement to a conflict which had, by then, degenerated into a bloody stalemate.

The subsequent significance of the AG was disproportionate to its small size (six personnel with a maximum possible deployment of twelve).[39] In 1995, Yuri Ushakov, Director for European Co-operation in the Russian Foreign Ministry, argued that:

Interaction within the OSCE on Chechen affairs is an unprecedented instance of openness on the part of a great power, of its
readiness to proceed in situations particularly complicated and
delicate from the point of view of international politics in strict
accordance with its obligations and to help consolidate the Organisation . . . The OSCE has set an important precedent. From now
on, drawing the Organisation into the solution of daunting problems in the event of a similar crisis in some other country . . . will
be not so much a question of the political will of the country
concerned as a common cause of all OSCE members relying on
past experience. Not all countries realise how difficult it is to open
oneself to such cooperation.[40]

Ushakov was, undoubtedly, striving to portray his country in the best
possible light here, but his evaluation is worthy of serious consideration. Russia had set a potentially significant precedent amongst major
member states by accepting an OSCE mission on its own territory,
although not one that has, in practice, as yet been followed by other
leading members.

Although the presence and activities of the AG in Chechnya by no
means put an end to allegations about human rights abuses being
committed by the Russian military,[41] a fundamental principle of the
OSCE was being strengthened nonetheless. This dates back to the
Basket Three human rights dimension of the original Helsinki agreements of 1975, as developed at subsequent summits and ministerial
meetings. All OSCE member states have formally accepted that their
behaviour towards their own people, including 'national minorities'
within their borders, is something in which the OSCE has a legitimate
interest.

Why did the Yeltsin government decide (not, reportedly, without
some 'difficulty'[42]) to allow an OSCE team into Chechnya? Two main
reasons are apparent. First, despite its strong focus in the mid-to-late
1990s on NATO enlargement, the Russian government evidently did
not want to see the pan-European framework being completely over-
shadowed and sidelined. The OSCE is the only European security
structure in which the Soviet Union and subsequently Russia have been
full and active members from the beginning. As such it provides Russia
with a seat at the table in European security affairs. It has not been the
only such seat, to be sure,[43] but it has been an important one nonetheless; a fact sometimes overlooked by western governments with a
greater portfolio of institutional memberships than the Russians.

Second, the break-up of the Soviet Union in 1991 left around

25 million ethnic Russians or Russian speakers living outside the borders of the Russian Federation itself. During the early 1990s, Russian leaders saw the CSCE/OSCE and other international organisations negotiating with the Baltic States on the status of the Russians living within their borders. Both the Estonian and Latvian governments agreed to amend elements of their domestic legislation which were deemed discriminatory against ethnic Russians and Russian speakers. It can be argued, therefore, that Russian leaders accepted their own 'Chechen precedent' as a *quid pro quo* and that they also saw it as a means to facilitate future OSCE interventionary activity, if necessary, in other places where the rights of local Russians might be threatened.

When conflict flared up for a second time in and around Chechnya from the late summer of 1999, the Russian government again initially demonstrated a concern to ensure that the OSCE was seen to be involved, even though the Assistance Group itself had temporarily withdrawn in December of the previous year.[44] In November 1999, Vladimir Putin, then the Russian Prime Minister, agreed that OSCE representatives could visit civilians displaced by the renewed violence into neighbouring areas and also 'liberated' areas of Chechnya itself. In this way, according to *Nezavisimaya Gazeta*, Russia could demonstrate 'that it isn't backing off from co-operation and doesn't intend to "hide corpses" '.[45] At the same time, *Noviye Izvestia* saw a bigger picture:

> Moscow is very concerned about the OSCE's diminishing role in European security in the wake of the Kosovo conflict. For one thing, the OSCE, in which Russia occupies an important place, could eventually be supplanted by the military organization that is now being put together in the EU – an organization whose door is closed to Moscow. By letting the OSCE into its own conflict zone, Russia staked out a good opening position for the Istanbul talks [the upcoming OSCE summit].[46]

As was perhaps to be expected at a time of renewed conflict, the Istanbul summit in November 1999 was preceded by strongly worded statements from Russian leaders and officials indicating that they would not tolerate 'interference' in Russia's 'internal affairs'.[47] At the summit itself, however, the Russian position was more moderate. True, there was evidence of disagreement over how Chechnya should be dealt with in the final agreed statement, with the result being that its signing was delayed. When it was signed, however, it was clear that the status quo ante, in terms of the OSCE presence there, had been upheld.

The Istanbul summiteers pacified their Russian partners by declaring that 'we strongly reaffirm that we fully acknowledge the territorial integrity of the Russian Federation and condemn terrorism in all its forms'. On the other hand, Russia agreed with 'the need to respect OSCE norms' and pledged that it would endeavour to create 'appropriate conditions for international organizations to provide humanitarian aid'. Further, it was agreed that 'a political solution is essential, and . . . the assistance of the OSCE would contribute to achieving that goal'. Overall, the Istanbul summit declaration reaffirmed 'the existing mandate of the OSCE Assistance Group in Chechnya'.[48]

In providing an overall summary at the end of the 1990s, Dov Lynch argued that:

> After 1994–6, Russian ambitions regarding the OSCE were directly linked to the issue of NATO enlargement. However, the Russian authorities have also increasingly perceived the importance of the organization in its own right as a means to institutionalize Russian involvement in wider European security discussions, and, perhaps more fundamentally, as a mechanism to address some of the security predicaments faced by Russia in Europe and the F[ormer]S[oviet]U[nion].[49]

It was, therefore, a disappointment to those who agreed with these sentiments when the AG's mandate in Chechnya was not renewed at the end of 2002. The Russian government, under President Vladimir Putin, blocked renewal, reportedly because it wished to restrict the OSCE's role to the provision of humanitarian relief whilst pursuing its own 'political process'. There were also allegations from prominent Russian officials and analysts that AG personnel had not been completely objective and dispassionate in their assessments of the humanitarian situation in Chechnya. The then Foreign Minister, Igor Ivanov, further suggested that the need for an OSCE presence had diminished as the situation in Chechnya 'was returning to normal'.[50]

Why had the Russian government allowed the OSCE's mandate to lapse and, in effect, thus forced it out of Chechnya? By late 2002, it was refocusing its priorities away from that organisation. Russia was in the process of finally becoming a full member of the Group of Eight (G8) leading industrial states. More pertinently to Europe, it had established a new forum for consultation and, crucially, some degree of joint decision making with NATO and its members. This was the NATO–Russia Council, established in May 2002 and discussed more fully in Chapter 5.

On this reading, the termination of the OSCE presence in Chechnya, whilst undoubtedly representing a blow for the organisation (and, arguably, for the humanitarian cause in that war-torn region), did not mean that the Russian government was turning its back on the rest of the world, or the West *per se*. In the long run, the decision may prove to be most significant as a milestone in the story of official Russian policy specifically towards the pan-European process.[51]

Looking at the period since 1991 as a whole, to what extent has the CSCE/OSCE served to anchor Russia in some kind of actual 'Common European Home'? Despite its role and achievements in the Baltics, Chechnya and elsewhere, the prevalent Russian view was probably best expressed by analyst Sergei Rogov in *Moskovskiye Novosti* in November 1999:

> The OSCE has not become the central structure for European security, as was planned during the Gorbachev era. Instead, the OSCE has turned into a discussion club, a vegetative organization with good intentions. The real force on the European continent is NATO (in the military sphere) and the European Union (in the economic sphere) ... It turns out that the common European home that Gorbachev spoke of has been built, but so far there's no place in it for us. This is a very unpleasant result, not only for us but for Europe as well.[52]

In this view, Russian relations with NATO are clearly of fundamental importance and they form the focus of analysis in the chapters that follow. Before getting down to these detailed discussions, however, it is instructive to consider how and in what ways it can be argued – as Rogov does – that a Common European Home has, in fact, been built. This is the focus for the discussions in the remainder of the current chapter.

The 'security' and 'civic' community in Europe

The year 1957 saw the publication of *Political Community and the North Atlantic Area*. This book explained the results of a study by a group of scholars working at Princeton University, led by Karl Deutsch, into the then novel concept of international 'security communities'. The term was used by the Princeton team to describe a situation where 'there is real assurance that the members of [the] community will not fight each other physically, but will settle their disputes in some other way'.[53] Two main types of potential security community were identified. 'Amalgamated' security communities exist, argued the Princeton team, when distinct units are welded together by a supranational authority, as is the case in the relationship between the constituent states and the federal government in the United States. 'Pluralistic' security communities exist when units (that is, states) retain substantial elements of sovereignty but, nevertheless, develop relations that effectively lead to the elimination of war as an instrument of their policies *vis-à-vis* each other.

In 1957, the Princeton scholars argued that war *had* become inconceivable between certain states, such as Canada and the US and the US and the UK. There were concerns about the future of the Federal Republic of Germany (FRG); at that time a NATO member of just three years' standing.[54] Overall, they argued that the 'North Atlantic Area' (which they defined as embracing not just the then NATO members but also Cold War neutrals in Europe) was a less demanding 'political community' at that time. This, they defined as a 'social group ... with a process of political communication, some machinery for enforcement, and some popular habits of compliance', although 'a political community is not necessarily able to prevent war within the area it covers'.[55]

In assessing the nature and extent of any 'community' that may exist in Europe today, it is helpful here to distinguish between the original notion of security community, as defined by the Princeton team in 1957, and what Michael Brenner has more recently termed a 'civic community' – although the two may be regarded as being inter-related.

A civic community has a more explicit normative basis, being premised on shared principles, standards and values that help to shape the policies and postures of participating states. Deutschian security communities, as Brenner puts it, can reflect 'merely the calculated preference of states'.[56] The existence of a *normative* community can alter state behaviour in more permanent and fundamental ways. Thus, its existence can bring about a situation where 'members entertain dependable expectations of peaceful change', as Emanuel Adler and Michael Barnett have put it.[57] The systemic changes that have occurred since the end of the Cold War in 1989–91 offer a good initial backdrop against which to assess the nature and scope of the community that actually exists in contemporary Europe.

The existence of a normative community is predicated, as noted, on *lasting* changes in the behaviour of participating states. In this context, Tom Lansford has developed the useful concept of what he calls 'the memberstate' (*sic*). According to Lansford, a memberstate 'is one that has subordinated aspects of [its sovereign] autonomy to ...

international norms and rules through efforts to harmonize relation-ships with international regimes. The drive for harmonization can cause a regime's norms and rules to be internalized by a state'.[58] In this context, the role of international institutions and organisations can be very important in bringing about and perpetuating the requisite changes in state behaviour.[59] It is no coincidence that Europe has been the arena within which the most developed and mature security com-munity in the world has grown and that it has also produced two of the world's most important international institutions – the European Union and NATO.

The security community dimension

For the kind of security community envisaged by Deutsch and his colleagues to exist, war must be both *structurally* and *conceptually* impossible amongst involved states. The states that form a security community should, therefore, first be incapable of mounting military operations against one another; the so-called 'structural incapacity to attack'. Second, their leaders should share a – probably unwritten but nonetheless solid and general – understanding that war would never be considered against other states within the security community however serious and protracted disputes with them may become.

Structural incapacity for offensive operations could, in theory, be attained in two ways. One would be to integrate the armed forces of participating states so comprehensively that it would become phys-ically impossible for any national leader to detach 'their' forces for separate operations either against neighbours and allies or anywhere else. This, indeed, was the kind of root-and-branch military integra-tion envisaged in the plans for a European Defence Community (EDC) amongst West European states in the early 1950s. Had these been adopted, they would likely have led to the appointment of a European defence minister and to the establishing of a common defence budget, for example.

A second, and perhaps more realistic, way in which a structural incapacity to attack could be entrenched would involve participating states adopting the principles of 'Non Offensive Defence' (NOD).[60] As its name suggests, NOD thinking boils down to support for the prop-osition that involved states should eschew both weapons systems and military concepts and tactics which give them the option to attack and conduct offensive military operations beyond their own borders.

Such ideas were highly controversial during the Cold War period and were criticised for potentially dangerously constraining NATO's options for responding to a Soviet attack, without necessarily increasing its ability to deter such an attack. Others argued that it was, in any event, not easy to define and agree on either types of weaponry or military tactics which were exclusively defensive and would be accepted as such by all relevant governments.[61] Finally, it should be borne in mind that security communities need not necessarily be pacific *per se*. Their existence merely ensures that military action *amongst involved states* is ruled out. Involved states may well wish to retain offensive military capabilities for dealing with prospective or actual *outside* threats and risks.

A structural incapacity to attack is certainly not present today amongst all members of the security community that undoubtedly exists in Europe. In terms of the size and capabilities of their armed forces, France and the UK can mount significant offensive operations if they want to, as the UK did in Iraq in 2003. In military terms, the FRG could too, though here the picture is somewhat more complicated because of historical and, until relatively recently, constitutional considerations.

What, then, can be said about the state of affairs on the conceptual side? Is it credible to believe that 'memberstates' would ever seriously consider going to war against a fellow NATO or EU member or, conversely, feel threatened by the prospect of military attack from their allies or partners? The bottom line is, of course, that no NATO or EU member has gone to war with another member since the institutions were first established in 1949 and 1957 respectively, nor, with the exception of the Greece–Turkey situation inside NATO, ever seriously threatened to do so.

One recently popular explanatory theory for this phenomenon is a variant of the view that shared norms and values have helped to modify traditionally competitive relations amongst states in Western Europe and North America. It focuses on the so-called 'democratic peace'. Democratic peace theory draws heavily upon West European and North American experiences for empirical support of its basic proposition that mature democracies do not go to war with one another.[62] One might expect greater historical support for this view with reference to the EU rather than to NATO, given that the latter, for much of its history, did not insist *de facto* that all its member states be mature democracies. Thus, tensions between Greece and Turkey may be ascribed to the long-time failure to establish a mature democracy in the latter state. In the military sphere, this is most particularly evident in the influence that the Turkish armed forces have continued to wield on its institutions of government.

Another popular explanation for the absence of war amongst NATO/EU members emphasises the role of increasing interdependence. According to this view in its simplest forms, the greater the network of ties and contacts between states, especially in the economic and commercial arenas, the lower the risk of war. This is because these states will have come to depend increasingly on one another for supplies of vital materials and for export markets and will not wish to see their access to these disrupted by turmoil or conflict.

Although the connection between interdependence and peace might, thus, appear to be self-evident, it should not necessarily be assumed that this is so. As John Lewis Gaddis has reminded us, there is little historical support for the assertion that relations of interdependence *automatically* promote international peace and stability. Gaddis makes his point by citing the specific examples of the economic interdependence that existed amongst the major powers in Europe on the eve of the First World War. He also notes that the US was Japan's largest trading partner on the eve of the Pearl Harbor attack in December 1941.[63]

Since the 1970s, Robert Keohane and Joseph Nye have developed the concept of what they call *complex* interdependence. They argue that, in a few regions of the world (again, mainly Western Europe and North America), relations of interdependence have come to be characterised by an especially dense web of connections, links and ties. These provide for contact and communication not only between governments but also between a range of other interest groups, lobbies and individuals within wider societies. The role of international institutions and organisations is, in the view of Keohane and Nye, very important in providing forums for communication and co-operation and also in norm setting. Institutions and organisations thus help to develop and maintain a co-operative culture amongst participants, helping to turn them into Lansfordian memberstates. Keohane and Nye also argue that, because the web joining certain states and societies together has become so dense, distinctions between military, economic and political issues have become increasingly blurred. As a consequence, military power is no longer seen as the final arbiter of disputes and disagreements in regions where complex interdependence exists.[64] In this way, it can be argued that complex interdependence acts as an essential underpinning to the creation and maintenance of a Deutschian security community.

Jaap de Wilde has, however, cautioned that the mere existence of interdependence, of whatever kind, neither presumes nor leads to equality between states. As a result, the potential for conflict remains and may even increase as two or more unequal states are drawn ever closer together. What really matters, in de Wilde's view, are *perceptions*. Citing other writers, he elaborates on this point:

> Since 1945 the Western democracies seemed to have learned the lesson. Marshall aid was offered and within a few years the enemy states were accepted as equal partners in all kinds of international organizations. Mutual interests outweighed national sentiments. Russett and Starr affirm that this had more to do with the perception of interdependence (the psychological dimension, as they call it) than with the mere facts of interdependence. Much of what is being seen as interdependence is not new, but is just being recognized for the first time. The 'material' facts of interdependence do not necessarily make for peace by themselves; the 'immaterial' facts must be present as well.[65]

The essential foundations of the contemporary security community in Europe are the perceptions of interdependence which have developed amongst those states (and societies) that make up its institutional core; that is, the members of NATO and the EU. Relations within Western Europe and North America and between the two represent the closest that any group of states has yet come to developing a mature and permanent international security community.

Is it correct to speak of this as being an essentially 'European' – rather than 'Atlantic' – community? Some analysts believe so. John Holmes, a former American diplomat, has argued that:

> The idea of Europe as a community has flourished, and the cohabitation of the Western European nations within the European Union (EU) has reached the point that separation, much less divorce, seems impossible. In contrast, could the fifty-year-old relationship between Europe and the United States come to an end? Yes, though not immediately, and not inevitably.[66]

Holmes thus implies that the United States' place in the security community has not been as strongly cemented as that of the West European participants. Others have argued, however, that such views seriously undervalue the United States' pivotal and continuing role as what Josef Joffe has called 'Europe's pacifier'. During the Cold War, it performed this role by extending a security guarantee, backed in the final analysis by nuclear weapons, to its NATO allies and also by taking on the role of NATO's leader. As Joffe puts it: 'by extending its guarantee, the United States removed the prime structural cause of conflict among [NATO] states – the search for an autonomous defense policy'. Further:

> By sparing the West Europeans the necessity of autonomous choice in matters of defense, the United States removed the systemic cause of conflict that had underlain so many of Europe's past wars (World War I is perhaps the best example.) By protecting Western Europe against others, the United States also protected the half-continent against itself. And by paving the way from international anarchy to security community the United States not only defused ancient rivalries but also built the indispensable foundation for future cooperation.[67]

That, it might be argued, was way back then. Yet, the United States continued to play a pacifying role among its allies during the 1990s. This was most clearly seen in the context of relations between Greece and Turkey. In 1996, the US took the lead in defusing heightened tensions between the two, which some had thought might actually lead to war, over disputed islets in the Aegean Sea. The then Assistant Secretary of State, Richard Holbrooke, the American mediator, played up the US role when he reportedly accused European Union members of 'literally sleeping through the night' as the US worked to defuse the crisis.[68] The following year, then Secretary of State Madeleine Albright reportedly engaged in 'more than a week of quiet shuttle diplomacy' in order to persuade Greek and Turkish leaders to agree to a joint confidence-building statement at a NATO summit in Madrid.[69] The US was also instrumental in leading the NATO actions which, in 1995 and 1999, brought peace, at least of a kind, to Bosnia and Kosovo respectively.

To imply, therefore, that the role of the United States is some kind of optional extra in the 'European' security community is unjustified. Whilst its role, arguably, is not quite as fundamental as it was during the Cold War, it is still key, not least because of its continuing status as the leader of NATO.

The civic community dimension

The core feature of a civic community, as defined earlier, is the role played by shared norms, values and standards of behaviour. Those most often described in the Atlantic and European context are individual freedom, political democracy and the rule of law. A second important feature is that the contemporary civic community, with which we are concerned here, is distinctively Atlanticist in nature.

There are two main schools of thought connected with this latter element. What may be called the *broad sweep* school identifies the existence of underlying common outlooks and shared viewpoints between West Europeans and North Americans based, as Christopher Layne has written, on 'the friendship and web of historical, political, and cultural ties' amongst peoples on the two continents.[70] For commentators like Layne, the existence of particular international institutions, such as NATO, is not necessary for this underlying community of shared beliefs and values to be maintained. Layne, indeed, has argued that 'Atlanticism' could survive even if NATO itself were wound up.

Contrasting with this, the second school of thought is *NATO-focused*. Adherents of this view argue that NATO, if not the sole repository of the values of the Atlantic civic community, does at least represent their most important institutional embodiment. Michael Brenner and Thomas Risse-Kappen, amongst others, have developed arguments along these lines. Brenner has called NATO an 'incorporated partnership', explaining the term thus:

> Incorporation has carried the allies beyond policy parallelism or ad hoc collaboration to concert ... Moreover, the articles of incorporation stipulate fixed obligations of the signatory states, establish routine procedures for consultation and joint decision making, and create mechanisms for review and oversight of actions taken. NATO structures are the organizational expression of those undertakings. They provide the staff, the integrated commands, the facilities and resources for carrying out missions. A political culture has evolved around them with a distinct set of norms and expectations. They counter the disposition of member governments to rethink the exceptional commitments that they have made.[71]

Risse-Kappen has argued in similar vein. In his view, NATO is of prime importance because 'as an institution [it] is explicitly built around norms of democratic decision-making, that is, nonhierarchy, frequent consultation implying co-determination, and consensus-building. Its institutional rules and procedures are formulated in such a way as to allow the allies to influence each other'.[72] The major part of *Cooperation Among Democracies*, Risse-Kappen's seminal work in this area, is devoted to a series of case studies demonstrating the extent to which the European NATO members were able to influence US foreign policy decision making through the NATO structures at key junctures during the Cold War. Brenner has also stressed the importance of this factor, writing that:

> [T]he culture of multilateralism [within NATO] eases the apprehensions of weaker states about possible domination by the stronger. The consensus rule amplifies the voice of the weaker; it opens opportunity for resisting the will of the stronger – especially that of the United States as the overwhelmingly most powerful and acknowledged leader of the Alliance.[73]

In summary: the discussions in this section so far support the view that there is a security community in existence today, embracing the NATO members (excluding Greece and Turkey at the moment). It is not restricted to the European landmass. The United States and Canada are both included with the former in an indispensable role. Indeed, an important part of the official ideology that has underpinned NATO has been that the US is 'a European power'.[74] This lends weight to the contention made by Adler and Barnett that regions such as 'Europe' are, in this context, primarily social rather than geographical constructs.[75]

The security community, in the original and relatively restricted sense in which Karl Deutsch and his colleagues defined the term in the 1950s, is today supplemented and underpinned by a civic community embodying shared norms and values. In order to be accepted into the community, therefore, in addition to eliminating use of the military instrument in relations with its partners, a state's political culture needs to firmly absorb and inculcate these core norms.

A growing community?

The community has never been a *pan*-European one. Despite its comprehensive membership, stretching from 'Vancouver to Vladivostok', the OSCE does not (yet) qualify as either a security or a civic community, as Michael Mihalka has argued, for two reasons. First, armed conflict and the use of military force cannot be ruled out in relations amongst its East European members. Second, as Mihalka puts it, 'the OSCE is more like a bazaar than a factory – states and international organizations can pick and choose how they wish to cooperate'.[76] It is true that, since the end of the Cold War, the OSCE has increasingly developed a role in establishing norms of behaviour on, for example, adopting democratic political systems for its member states and, further, in monitoring their compliance with the norms. Yet, this putative international regime is, in practice, still felt to be essentially non-binding in many parts of the OSCE area.

Pál Dunay has suggested that, in reality, post-Cold War Europe has been divided into three distinct areas.[77] In Western Europe, first, Dunay agreed with most other observers that an established security and civic community exists. Put another way, this is the site of the actually existing Common European Home, perceived by Sergei Rogov and others.

In Central Europe, which Dunay defined as the non-Soviet former Warsaw Pact states or their successors, together with the three Baltic States and Slovenia, there have been, in his view, clear indications of an *emerging* community since the mid 1990s. The indications have been evident in, for example, the extent to which states in the region have sought to tackle problems and disputes with neighbours by non-military means.[78] Dunay also emphasised the fact that every one of these states indicated a desire to join the EU and NATO during the 1990s. By the middle of 2004, all of them had actually joined at least one – and usually both – of the core European institutions.[79]

The third and final area in Dunay's typology is Eastern Europe. For him this label embraces Russia, the remaining former Soviet republics and the successor states of the former Yugoslavia with the exception of Slovenia. All of these states have either been engaged in armed conflict of various kinds or else have been in situations of tension with one or more of their neighbours, which could potentially erupt into war.

Against this overall backdrop, Dunay has argued that 'what we should aim at in Europe is not the unification of the old continent but a redrawing of the dividing lines. The reason for not unifying Europe is not that there are forces which oppose unification, it is rather that the developments of recent years have proved that *unification is impossible*' [emphasis in the original].[80]

If this proposition is accepted, the prospects for a fully pan-European 'Common Home' being constructed are, at best, remote. What, then, can Russia – as the core part of Dunay's 'Eastern Europe' – realistically hope for in terms of its relations with NATO and its members? The arguments developed in the remainder of this volume suggest that governments and leaders in both Russia and the West have accepted, at least on a rhetorical level, that the development of *partnership* between them is the best realistic goal. Yet, this objective in itself has often proved contentious. As the discussions in the following chapters suggest, there has not, to date, been a fundamental agreement between Russian and western leaders (nor, indeed, within the Russian government and amongst western governments) on what 'partnership' actually means.

2 Dramatis Personae
Russia and NATO since 1991

Introduction

Before embarking on a detailed analysis of the course of relations between NATO and Russia in the years since 1991, it will be useful and instructive to, first, consider the nature and character of both of these actors, in so far as these have influenced their actions in the foreign policy arena, most particularly *vis-à-vis* each other. The discussions in this chapter, therefore, are intended to fulfil an important scene-setting function, by enabling the reader to better understand the forces, agendas and impulses that have contributed to the formation of policy and attitudes on each side.

NATO refocused: before September 11 2001

During the 1990s, the North Atlantic Treaty Organisation was significantly re-oriented and re-tooled. Broadly speaking, this reinvention process proceeded in four main areas, according to NATO's own terminology and definitions: 'internal adaptation', 'external adaptation', the adoption of 'peace support' roles and, finally, growing involvement in 'crisis management and crisis response' operations.

Internal adaptation

Internal adaptation has been NATO-speak for the restructuring and reforms that have focused on rebalancing relations between member states. During the controversies over NATO enlargement in the 1990s, many, especially on the opposing side, expected that taking in new members would be bound to have implications for NATO's established decision-making procedures. Opponents charged that consensus-based decision making in NATO would become difficult, if not impossible, as new members, unversed in such techniques, were signed up.[1] Since enlargement actually began in 1999, however, there has been little obvious impact on NATO decision making. The controversies over Iraq in 2002 and 2003 were, fundamentally, amongst original and long-standing members: that is, the US and UK on one side, and France and the FRG on the other.

The more important elements of the NATO internal adaptation process, in practice, have been the discussions and studies focusing on the possibility of creating mechanisms whereby European members of the alliance might undertake military operations without the frontline participation of US forces. All members have been committed to this in principle since January 1994 when, at a summit meeting in Brussels, outline agreement was reached on establishing so-called Combined Joint Task Forces (CJTF). The idea, as expressed in official NATO statements, was that flexible military forces could be deployed on 'non-Article Five operations'[2] by a 'coalition of the willing'. In practice, therefore, not all NATO members would actually take part, although there was a presumption that all would approve the overall political and strategic goals of a CJTF mission.

Over the remainder of the 1990s, the CJTF concept was developed on paper and in official rhetoric to the extent that a potential relationship between NATO and an increasingly militarised European Union began to seem both possible and desirable. At the NATO Washington summit in April 1999, it was officially agreed that NATO members, including the US, were 'ready to define and adopt the necessary arrangements for ready access by the European Union to the collective assets and capabilities of the Alliance, for operations in which the Alliance as a whole is not engaged militarily as an Alliance'.[3] This outline offer was taken as significant encouragement by those in favour of proceeding with the development of an 'autonomous' EU military capability.[4] Yet, it largely remained confined to the realms of paper declarations and planning, notwithstanding the EU members' own declared intention, later in 1999, to put in place some real military capability by the year 2003.[5] Overall, the internal adaptation, relatively speaking, has remained the least practically developed of the four elements of NATO's adaptation, both before and after the events of September 11 2001.[6]

External adaptation

External adaptation is a term that refers, fairly obviously, to relations between NATO and non-member states (specifically in Europe).[7] It has embraced five main elements, of which the first four are directly relevant to the issue of Russia–NATO relations. The overall framework for NATO's external adaptation has, since 1994, been provided by the Partnership for Peace (PfP) process, which is discussed further, in the Russia–NATO context, in Chapter 3. A key subset of this has been, second, the NATO enlargement process. During the 1990s, this was the most significant and enduring bone of contention in Russia–NATO relations, as the discussions in Chapter 3 will also demonstrate. Attempts to set the Russia–NATO relationship, specifically, on a stable footing have constituted the third element of the external adaptation. In addition to its efforts to forge an enduring partnership with Russia, since 1997 NATO has also been developing what has officially been called a 'distinctive partnership' with the Ukraine.[8] Hitherto, this has not caused any significant complications for the Russia–NATO relationship. It is, however, possible that Ukraine–NATO relations could become more of an issue for Russian leaders in future if initial indications of an interest in pursuing eventual NATO membership for Ukraine are followed up by its own leadership.[9]

The final element of NATO's external adaptation, which should be mentioned briefly here, concerns the relationship between NATO and the traditional neutral states in Europe: Finland, Sweden, Austria, Switzerland and Eire. For much of the time since the early 1990s, there seemed to be little requirement for NATO to treat these states distinctively. All had joined PfP at a fairly early stage after its inception in January 1994 and their governments seemed largely content with what NATO had to offer there. In addition, they proved willing to contribute to NATO-led peace support operations in Bosnia and Kosovo. Since the NATO enlargement process got underway, however, and most especially since the second enlargement round, which entailed seven new members joining at the same time during 2004, the neutrals have increasingly been left as the most significant group of non-NATO member states within the PfP. This has started to provoke questions about what these states might expect and demand from PfP in future, and even about whether some of them might seriously consider the possibility of NATO membership.[10]

Peace support

NATO and its member states were effectively propelled into a largely unplanned role in peace support and related operations by the bloody disintegration of Yugoslavia, in particular the civil war in Bosnia, in the early 1990s. During the course of 1992, members stated that they were prepared, in principle, to support peacekeeping and related operations under the auspices of the (then) CSCE or the United Nations. Then UN Secretary-General, Boutros Boutros-Ghali, responded to this offer with alacrity and, over a two-year period from the summer of 1992, NATO collective military planning and command resources, as well as troops from many of its member states, were deployed to Bosnia. NATO also played the central role in implementing the military tasks of the Dayton peace accords for Bosnia from January 1996 until December 2004, when an EU-led force took over.[11] A NATO-led peace support operation remains ongoing in Kosovo, where it has been deployed since June 1999. Its initial deployment followed the coerced agreement of the then Yugoslav President, Slobodan Milosevic, in the face of Operation Allied Force, the NATO bombing campaign which will be discussed, in the Russia–NATO context, in Chapter 4.

Crisis management and response

When, in March 1999, NATO members launched Operation Allied Force against the Serbs – controversially without seeking a mandate from the UN Security Council – they confirmed, *de facto*, a fourth major role for the alliance. This was to stand ready to use military power coercively, as well as for peace support purposes, on non-Article Five operations. Contrary to popular belief, the Kosovo air campaign was not the first occasion on which they had done this. Operation Deliberate Force, a campaign of NATO airstrikes against Bosnian Serb military forces in August–September 1995, had helped pave the way for the end of the civil war in Bosnia and for the Dayton agreements. Nevertheless, once it became clear that President Milosevic was not going to concede quickly to NATO's demands over Kosovo in the spring of 1999, and that Operation Allied Force would thus have to continue indefinitely, NATO members evidently decided that some *post facto* justification for it was required. They attempted to supply this by formally adopting – at their Washington summit, which took place in the middle of the bombing campaign – the new role of undertaking what they called crisis management and crisis response operations.

By the end of the 1990s, as a consequence of its members' decisions to permit NATO to become involved in peace support and crisis management operations in South East Europe, it could reasonably be argued that traditional Cold War distinctions between in- and out-of-area competencies for NATO within the wider European context had been rendered moot.[12] This was an important development, given the extent to which these had appeared to be set in stone as recently as 1990–1.

In addition to the problems caused by NATO's decision to proceed with eastward enlargement, it was disputes over the decision to use military force during the Kosovo crisis, without specific UN sanction, that caused the most turbulence and controversy in Russia–NATO relations during the 1990s, as discussed in Chapter 4. How and why a terminal rupture in relations was avoided, and a process of repair begun, even during the NATO bombing campaign itself, are amongst the issues that will be addressed in Chapter 4, and also in the first section of Chapter 5.

NATO challenged? September 11 and beyond

In the period since the terrorist attacks on New York and Washington on September 11 2001, there has been speculation in some quarters that NATO's days as a significant international security institution might finally be numbered.[13] Two main arguments have been advanced in support of this proposition. The first concerns the immediate aftermath of the attacks and the alleged failure of the unprecedented invocation of Article Five of the NATO treaty to produce genuinely united and multinational action. The second – more long-term – criticism has been focused on NATO's alleged irrelevance in the ongoing US-led 'war on terror', as it has unfolded in Afghanistan and Iraq since 2001.

Article Five was formally invoked for the first time in the alliance's history in September/October 2001. Anne Deighton has expressed a common view, both in describing this as 'a crucial moment' and then proceeding to note that 'Article 5 failed to trigger a NATO-led military response'. This inaction, she asserts, 'exposed the conditional nature of Article 5'.[14] Former NATO Secretary-General Javier Solana was more candid in his reported assessment. He was quoted as saying that 'NATO invoked its most sacred covenant, that no one had dared touch in the past, and it was useless! Absolutely useless!'[15] In similar vein, the then Secretary-General, Lord Robertson, 'and the whole NATO establishment' were reported to have been 'flabbergasted' by the alleged lack of US response to the invocation of Article Five.[16]

Hindsight and a more dispassionate analytical approach both suggest that these views are overblown. To begin with, the precedent-setting significance of the invocation of Article Five under the circumstances pertaining in the immediate aftermath of September 11 should not be overlooked. This was not purely or mainly symbolic, as is sometimes suggested. As Philip Gordon notes, 'with very little public or official debate, NATO had now interpreted Article Five to include a terrorist attack on a member state'.[17] This was a contingency that was not remotely in the minds of those who drafted the NATO treaty back in the 1940s.[18]

The situation was, perhaps, not quite as clear-cut as Gordon suggests. The initial invocation of Article Five, in a NATO statement issued on 12 September 2001, was qualified by the inclusion of the following phrase: 'if it is determined that this attack was directed from abroad against the United States'.[19] What this meant was that NATO member states were willing to consider themselves bound by the invocation of Article Five only if they were satisfied that *another state* had been involved, either in organising the September 11 attacks or in providing significant material support to those who had. Thus, there was a three-week gap between the September 12 statement and a declaration by Secretary-General Robertson that this criterion had been met and the Taliban regime in Afghanistan identified as the *de facto* sponsors of the Al-Qaeda movement.[20] Within days thereafter, the US began military operations in Afghanistan.

With regard to the supposed lack of collective military activity in the autumn of 2001, several points can be made. First, a package of eight measures *was* agreed under NATO auspices.[21] This package was broad in scope though, some argued, lacking in substance. The first point, for example, referred to enhanced intelligence sharing. Doubtless this was a highly desirable goal in the context of the nascent war on terror. NATO, however, had never been endowed with a significant intelligence-gathering and analysis dimension by its member states. Neither was it to acquire one in the weeks and months after September 11, not least because of continued US reluctance to share sensitive intelligence material even with its allies (with the exception of the UK). Other points in NATO's agreed package provided for seemingly commonsense measures which, presumably, would have been taken anyway in the wake of such significant and large-scale terrorist atrocities. Thus, point three called for 'measures to provide increased security for facilities of the United States and other Allies' on the territory of NATO members. Point five requested that members 'provide blanket over flight clearances for the United States and other Allies' aircraft', whilst point six requested 'access for the United States and other Allies to ports and airfields on the territory of NATO nations'.

The most important points, specifically, for NATO as an international security institution were the final two. Both of these mandated the creation and deployment of new multinational military operations. The seventh point provided for Operation Active Endeavour, which remains ongoing to the present day. This saw the deployment of the multinational NATO Standing Naval Forces to the Mediterranean in order to provide ongoing anti-terrorist patrols and release US ships for deployment elsewhere. The final point led to probably the most publicly high-profile of all the elements of the 'NATO' response to the events of September 11. This was Operation Eagle Assist – the deployment of NATO Airborne Early Warning planes to help patrol the airspace above the United States in order to release similar US national assets for alternative deployment.

There is certainly scope for differences of opinion over how significant this package was. For example, David Brown downplays it.[22] Philip Gordon, on the other hand, calls it 'a good demonstration of the value of political commitment and integrated and interoperable military forces' [as developed within the NATO framework].[23] To baldly assert, however, that the invocation of Article Five produced no 'NATO action' worthy of mention is both over-simplistic and inaccurate.

The precise terms in which Article Five is couched can usefully be recalled. This article states that:

> The Parties agree that an armed attack against one or more of them in Europe or North America shall be considered an attack against them all and consequently they agree that, if such an armed attack occurs, each of them, in exercise of the right of individual or collective self-defence recognised by Article 51 of the Charter of the United Nations, will assist the Party or Parties so attacked by taking forthwith, individually and in concert with the other Parties, such action as it deems necessary, including the use of armed force, to restore and maintain the security of the North Atlantic area.[24]

The basis of Article Five, as drafted, was the preservation of the decision-making rights of individual signatory states. This is evident in the inclusion of the phrases 'each of them', 'taking forthwith, individually and in concert with' and, perhaps most famously, 'such action as [each] deems necessary, including the use of armed force'. In theory, therefore, it would be possible for each signatory to decide to take no, or limited, military action in response to an armed attack against an ally. Although not stated explicitly, the correlation of this is that those attacked are not required to avail themselves of all the assistance offered.

During the Cold War, the relative looseness of the security guarantee offered by Article Five was purposely overlaid by NATO member states with what can be called the 'presumption of automaticity'. From the early 1950s, members created dense and demanding multinational structures and arrangements that were viewed as effectively guaranteeing that, at least those member states – primarily the US – which maintained military dispositions in the FRG, would effectively have no choice about becoming involved in repelling any Warsaw Pact attack. This conscious effort to create and lock in the presumption that a collective response to aggression would, in actuality, be automatic directly inspired most of the controversial elements of NATO's Cold War military strategy and doctrine: including forward defence, the notion of a 'tripwire' force and, not least, the refusal to rule out the possibility of the first use of theatre nuclear weapons.

Those who have argued that the invocation of Article Five in 2001 somehow resulted in a major NATO failure can be said to have harboured unrealistic expectations based on lingering Cold War assumptions. Many, including it would seem some prominent leaders and officials, such as Javier Solana, seemed to have anticipated a 'SACEUR-led military operation under the authority of the North Atlantic Council', as Philip Gordon puts it.[25] When that failed to materialise, some of them appear to have jumped to the conclusion that NATO therefore failed outright. What happened, in fact, was that NATO *did* respond collectively and with full US support, involvement and encouragement. It did not do so, however, in the way that some appear to have expected.

As noted earlier, the second argument advanced by those who have doubted NATO's utility in adapting to meet new challenges is centred chiefly on the build-up to, and aftermath of, the 2003 war in Iraq. During the former period in particular – most especially the early months of 2003 – the output of the professional commentariat was replete with headlines of the 'most serious crisis in NATO's history' variety.[26]

The alleged 'crisis' has not proved terminal, nor is it yet showing serious signs of doing so. Why is this? Some have argued that the crisis was not as serious as it may have appeared to be in the first place. It was to be expected that Secretary-General Robertson would subsequently eulogise upon the extent to which, even at the height of tensions, decisions on contentious issues – such as the deployment of air defence assets to Turkey – could still be taken, albeit with acrimony and delay.[27] However, some academic observers have also argued that the divisions amongst NATO members were not as sharp or as deep as they seemed.[28]

Certainly, since the Iraq war in March–April 2003, NATO members have made some significant collective decisions. Amongst these have been the agreement to place the International Security Assistance Force (ISAF) in Afghanistan directly under a multinational NATO command structure from August 2003 and to begin, albeit tentatively, to extend elements of the NATO presence in that country beyond Kabul from 2004. This set an important precedent. Afghanistan, for all the complaints about the inadequate strength and mandate of ISAF, represented the first occasion on which a formal NATO operation (that is, one conducted within its integrated command and planning framework) had taken place *outside Europe*. It thus opened up a new cut-of-area debate. The previous one, over whether or not NATO's collective assets and resources could be used for military operations beyond its members' borders *within* Europe, was, as noted earlier, effectively settled during the 1990s in Bosnia and Kosovo.

The period since 2004 has been marked by debates over the extent to which NATO collectively could and should get involved in international reconstruction efforts in Iraq. In what was, incidentally, a good example of how the NATO crisis 'industry' works, disagreements in the first half of 2004 between France and the US over the seemingly rather arcane question of whether NATO should offer to train Iraqi security personnel inside or outside that country were well publicised.[29] Once consensus was reached and an actual multinational NATO-led training capability began to be developed inside Iraq over the summer (with the option retained to conduct out-of-country training as well), media attention dropped off to such an extent that these developments went largely unreported.[30]

These developments, in themselves, do not guarantee NATO a stable and secure long-term future. To begin with, the moves made so far are fragile and tentative. The well-publicised arguments during 2004 over both the Iraq training and whether to make relatively modest augmentations to ISAF's functions and troop strength[31] testify to this. As such, this demonstrates that it is premature to speak of the creation of a solid and enduring acceptance of extra-European roles amongst NATO's members as a whole.

In consequence, and overall, there remains a sense that NATO cannot yet provide a *definitive* answer to the core question: about what it is for in the post-September 11 era.[32] As one prominent British analyst noted in May 2004, a paradoxical situation has pertained. NATO seems to be 'a bit lost in terms of its purpose, whilst at the same time being busier than at any time in its history'.[33] Others – more positively – have detected a sense that NATO might be on a cusp. This could potentially offer, as Paul Cornish puts it, 'a moment of great opportunity ... to structure the transatlantic security debate once and for all in NATO's favour, to show that a transformed NATO can meet the challenges of twenty-first-century security, and to prove NATO to be both militarily and politically indispensable'.[34]

It remains unclear whether such a rosy scenario, from NATO's perspective, is as yet in the process of being realised. Early in 2005, there was a burst of controversy following a speech delivered in the name of Gerhard Schröder, the German Chancellor. In his text, Schröder claimed that NATO was 'no longer the primary venue where transatlantic partners discuss and coordinate strategies'. This was not a call for the abolition of NATO, as Schröder's text made clear. He argued that 'the admission of new members is proof that NATO continues to be attractive' and, further, that 'NATO's presence in Afghanistan has highlighted how helpful its military organization can be even in distant crises'. What the Chancellor suggested was an eminent persons panel, to review what NATO was doing and make recommendations for future improvements.[35] A similar exercise had recently been carried out at the UN, at the instigation of Secretary-General Kofi Annan. Although the German leader was not, therefore, calling into question NATO's existence *per se*, the tone of his remarks, and the very fact that they had been prepared for delivery in the name of the leader of one of NATO's core member states, was sufficient to demonstrate that debates about NATO's future have by no means yet been permanently and decisively settled.

The re-emergence of Russia: foreign policy priorities

International power

Independent Russia was one of fifteen states – all of them former constituent republics of the Soviet Union – which emerged when the latter effectively fell apart in December 1991. Although the world's second superpower had thus disappeared, a clear majority of Russia's leaders, from across the political spectrum, continued to claim a status for their own state amongst the ranks of the world's leading powers.

This did not necessarily mean, however, that they conceived of Russia as being a superpower in the traditional Cold War sense.[36] In the early years of the new Russia's life, Andrei Kozyrev, its first Foreign Minister, generally preferred to use the term 'normal great power'. This asserted status was deliberately shorn of Soviet-style ideological claims.[37] In the mid 1990s, amidst indications of cooling relations between Russia and the United States, the term 'superpower' crept back into usage on occasion, even amongst relatively liberal members of the Russian elite, such as Kozyrev himself. In an article published in *Izvestia* in March 1994, for example, the then Foreign Minister wrote that 'Russia . . . will remain a superpower not only insofar as nuclear-missile and military might as a whole are concerned but also in space exploration and the creation of the latest technologies, not to mention in terms of natural resources and geostrategic position.' He added that, in terms of its relationship with the United States, Russia 'can only be an equal partner, not a junior one'.[38] Statements such as these carried clear echoes of the consistent desire of Soviet leaders to be accorded equal status in their Cold War bilateral relations with the United States. Russian leaders and officials thus tended to resort to use of the term 'superpower' specifically when they were speaking of relations with the US and at times when they perceived these relations to be undergoing strain.

Whether the specific term 'superpower' was used or not, most western analysts during the 1990s believed that what James Sherr called a 'great power ideology' continued to shape the views and attitudes of nearly all Russian leaders, and, indeed, many of those who themselves analysed and followed what Russia and its leaders did.[39] As the new millennium dawned, however, and the presidency of Boris Yeltsin gave way to that of Vladimir Putin, much of the commentary began to change in this key respect. In 2000, for example, Paula Dobriansky argued that, by then, there was 'no nostalgia for Moscow's superpower past' amongst Russian leaders, officials and analysts.[40] Meanwhile, former US Senator Sam Nunn, and Adam Stulberg, described Russia as a 'recovering great power [but] a weak federal state'.[41] In early 2001, Allen Lynch wrote that Russia was 'a large power rather than a great power'.[42]

These changing views amongst informed outside observers were undoubtedly inspired, in substantial part, by some evidence that Russian leaders themselves now seemed less certain about their country's actual status in the world. In a telling psychological point, Robert Legvold drew attention in 2001 to the tendency of official Russian foreign and security policy documents to habitually refer to Russia's supposed status as a great and influential global power. 'Russian leaders', Legvold argued, thus 'spend a fair amount of time reassuring themselves about the greatness and importance of their country'. He suggested that this reflected underlying doubts about its actual status: 'such preening is hard to imagine from, say, Berlin or Tokyo, but Moscow feels the need'.[43] In fairness, it could, of course, be argued that the ongoing diplomatic campaigns being pursued by both the FRG and Japan towards securing permanent seats on the United Nations Security Council have also been a form of 'preening', and one which Russia, as an existing permanent member, has had no need to engage in itself.

In terms of practical policy, two decisions by President Putin early in his first term, in 2001, were especially significant. These were to close both the Russian naval base at Cam Ranh Bay in Vietnam and an intelligence-gathering facility in Cuba.[44] Both of these had been major Soviet military facilities during the Cold War and had been retained by the Russians in the Yeltsin era. Their retention was perhaps due less to their ongoing military value than their political and symbolic importance in underpinning Russian claims to be a power with genuine global influence and presence. In addition, it was surely not coincidental that these facilities were in two states that raised particularly sensitive issues as far as US foreign policy was concerned.[45] The official reason given for Putin's decision to withdraw from Vietnam and Cuba was a purely economic one, but it was bound to be seen more widely, in some quarters, as representing tacit acceptance that Russia could and should no longer aspire to genuinely global power status.

In retrospect, however, it seems likely that Putin was purposely seeking to liquidate Cold War era commitments at an early stage in his presidency. This would free up resources to better concentrate on what he considered to be more relevant and hence more important issues and areas. In this context, it is possible to view his May 2003 'state of the nation' address as being significant. In it, the Russian President declared that:

> All our decisions and actions must be dedicated to ensuring that, in the foreseeable future, Russia will firmly take its place among the truly strong, economically advanced and influential states of the world. This is a qualitatively new task, a qualitatively new step for the country. A step which we were unable to take earlier because of a number, a multitude of pressing problems. We have this opportunity and we must take it.[46]

Thus, it can be argued that a number of decisions and actions since 2003 reflect an increasing sense of official self-confidence on the part of Russian leaders. Such decisions include: pressing ahead with the sale of nuclear technology to Iran, despite declared opposition from the US; refusing to contribute troops to the ongoing US-led coalition effort in Iraq; and the unprecedented public criticism of the OSCE, noted in Chapter 1 of this volume.[47]

Attempting to conceptualise such decisions and actions, in congressional testimony given in March 2005, noted analyst Celeste Wallander described the basis of the Putin foreign policy as 'essentially a 19th century European great power approach to security and diplomacy'. In her view, 'the Russian leadership understands and responds to 21st century threats in a great power and geopolitical framework in which the re-establishment of Russian power through economic growth and political relationships is paramount'.[48]

Thus, although the Cold War term 'superpower' is used relatively infrequently in official Russian circles today, this should not be taken to indicate acceptance on the part of the Russian leadership that their country is a reduced and limited regional power only. Under both the Yeltsin and Putin administrations, efforts have been made to develop what may be called multi-directional influence: that is, to balance relations with the US and Western European states by fostering 'strategic partnerships' with important states elsewhere, most especially in Asia.

Historically, as is well known, three core schools of thought have developed with regard to Russian foreign policy priorities: the 'Westernisers', the 'Slavophiles' and the 'Eurasianists'. The first school basically believes that Russia's vocation is to be a European power. As such, its adherents argue that Russia should aim to integrate itself to the greatest possible degree with 'the West' and measure its progress and development according to western norms and standards. The Slavophile school has rejected this and argues instead that Russia's true destiny and role is to be the leader of the Slavic nations in Eastern and South Eastern Europe. This makes it the narrowest of the ideologies in terms of geographical scope and focus. The Eurasianist school, finally, has articulated the broadest parameters. Its adherents have postulated ideas about a mutually reinforcing and balanced focus on Russia's relations with Asia, Europe and the United States.

Sergei Stankevich, a key adviser to President Yeltsin in the first part of the 1990s, distilled the essence of Eurasianist arguments into a number of related propositions. Whilst agreeing with Kozyrev and others that the 'messianic' (that is, overtly expansionist) elements of Soviet ideology should not be revived, Stankevich nevertheless argued that Russia's geopolitical position endowed it with a special 'mission' in the world. This mission was to act as a kind of bridge between the civilisations of Asia and the West: as Stankevich put it, 'to initiate and maintain a multilateral dialogue of cultures, civilizations and states'. He argued that discharging this mission effectively depended upon avoiding an over-concentration of Russian foreign policy effort on relations with the US and Europe, as he alleged Yeltsin and Kozyrev had been guilty of doing. On the other hand, he did not suggest the adoption of a hostile posture towards either the US or Europe. In what could be seen as a nod to Slavophile sentiment, Stankevich also maintained that Russia had a 'legitimate and natural' role in 'stabilising' relations between and within the other newly independent post-Soviet states. This role was especially important, he argued, in view of the presence of millions of ethnic Russians within the borders of these states.[49]

How influential have such ideas been on Russian policy makers? In the spring of 1992, Andrei Kozyrev wrote that 'Russia is a great . . . Eurasian power in all its aspects – European, Asian, Siberian and Far Eastern – a power that in its domestic life and foreign policy refutes the pessimistic prophecy of Rudyard Kipling that East and West will never meet.'[50] Contrary to the popular impression that the Yeltsin–Kozyrev team were overly pro-western during their first years in power, the Russian government displayed a distinct interest in Asian matters from the beginning. During the second half of 1992, for example, much of the Russian Foreign Ministry's time was taken up with the planning of an Asian grand tour for President Yeltsin. This was to take in South Korea, Japan, China and India. As an indication of the seriousness with which Yeltsin and his advisers viewed this trip, it emerged that they were apparently prepared to offer major concessions to the Japanese on the previously intractable problem of the disputed Kurile Islands. Situated off the northern tip of the main Japanese islands, the Kuriles had been occupied by Soviet/Russian forces since 1945, but had consistently been claimed by Japan. Opposition from nationalist opponents within Russia to any prospective deal forced Yeltsin to postpone the Japanese leg of his visit and, in the process, damaged his and Kozyrev's fledgling Asian strategy. Nevertheless, enough of it subsequently survived to demonstrate that a consistent effort to balance Russian policy between the West and Asia was being made.[51] From the mid 1990s to the present day, the main effort in this area has been the attempt to develop an enduring strategic partnership with China.[52] More sporadically, there has also been official Russian interest in developing a similar partnership with India.

There has, nevertheless, been a persisting sense in some quarters that the influence of Eurasianist ideas reflects the underlying weakness of Russia, rather than its strength. David Kerr has argued that important factors in making Russian leaders and officials receptive to such ideas have been, first, a perception of territorial vulnerability in the east of the country and the consequent desire to keep a wary eye on strategic and political developments within the states on Russia's eastern borders. On the other side, according to Kerr (and others), Russia has effectively been pushed eastwards by the loss of Soviet alliances in the former Eastern Europe and, subsequently, the collapse of the Soviet Union itself. According to this line of thinking, these developments have had the impact of physically separating Russia from the European mainstream.[53]

Other analysts and observers agree with Kerr that Russia and the countries of Asia are not, and have never been, natural allies or partners. Some have implied, therefore, that a foreign policy based on Eurasianist ideas is a second best option, to compensate for Russia's sometimes strained post-Cold War relations with Europe and the US, where its real interests nonetheless lay. Vladimir Baranovsky has put forward a particularly cogent argument along these lines. He has written that 'in terms of culture and civilization, the distance between Russia and Europe is meaningless in comparison with what separates Russia from Asia; [although] geopolitically Russia is undoubtedly in between the two'.[54] Jack Matlock, the last US Ambassador to the Soviet Union, has argued in a similar vein:

> Russia is a Eurasian power in the geographic sense, just as the United States is both an Atlantic and a Pacific power. But Russia is primarily a European power, and no amount of wishful thinking can enable it to play off the 'East' against the 'West'. Historically, it has had more conflicts with Islamic peoples than with Europeans, and it extorted much of its Asian territory from China; understandably, the Chinese and Islamic peoples of Central Asia have regarded Russians not as fellow Asians but as colonialists. The Japanese have viewed Russia as an imperial rival – one that even today occupies territories they consider rightfully theirs, notably the Kuril Islands. What can Russia offer any of these countries that they cannot obtain in greater abundance directly from the West? Russia will only doom itself to backwardness, stagnation, and worse if it distances itself from Europe in pursuit of some never-never alliance in the East.[55]

Although Eurasianist ideas appeared to be in vogue in certain quarters during the years immediately after 1991, they subsequently lost currency. By the turn of the millennium, according to Richard Sakwa, 'it was clear that Eurasianism had died, both intellectually and geopolitically [because] it was unable to sustain a coherent foreign policy'.[56] To be fair, foreign policy making in most states involves compromises between and amongst the views of various distinct groups and interests. Russia has been no exception in this respect. In 1993, for example, the first foreign policy concept for Russia was released. It had been put together with input from eight separate executive and parliamentary ministries and agencies. Pressure from lobbies and interest groups outside government, or with a foot in both camps (such as business leaders), further complicated the picture and has subsequently added to the difficulties of framing consistent and coherent Russian foreign and security policies.[57] Finally, it has been argued that key agencies in the foreign policy-making process, such as the Ministry of Foreign Affairs, have been internally divided to the extent that different departments within the ministry have, at times, effectively been pursuing 'their own foreign policy'.[58]

There have even been allegations that Russia, in effect, has had no foreign policy *per se*.[59] Accusations such as this take the argument too far. It is fairer to suggest that there has not always been a clear and consistent foreign policy line emanating from the Russian government. The problem has been that this failure on the part of the Russian foreign policy elite to pursue a consistently clear line on some issues has tended to produce stances and postures that have been counter-productively negative and reactive.[60] These factors have, arguably, added to perceptions that Russian foreign policy since the early 1990s has been substantially the product of weakness rather than strength.[61]

Russia and the other former Soviet states

Stephen Covington has argued that Russia has been pursuing what amounts to an 'insecurity policy', based on both its weakness relative to the US and its allies in Western Europe and on Russian leaders' concerns about their state's internal stresses and strains. According to Covington, the pursuit of such a policy helps to explain the emphasis that has been placed in Russian foreign policy on the other former Soviet states. Russia's leaders have wanted the states concerned to be closely bound to Russia, in order to both insulate it against feared western penetration and also to form a 'strategic corset' to help prevent possible disintegration of the Russian Federation itself.[62]

Russian policy towards the former Warsaw Pact states, and the former Soviet states (the latter in what Russians generally call the 'near abroad'),[63] has been of particular relevance and importance in helping to shape relations between Russia and NATO. This has been the case, most especially, in the context of Russian opposition to the eastward enlargement of NATO's membership during the 1990s, as discussed in Chapter 3.

With the Soviet Union about to be wound up in December 1991, President Yeltsin and his key advisers had been preoccupied with trying to salvage a Slavic core of states which would maintain a close association with Russia. To this end, only representatives of Ukraine and Belarus were invited by Russia to the initial meeting that established the Commonwealth of Independent States (CIS). Protests by leaders of Central Asian republics, especially the Kazakhs, soon forced a rethink. At a second meeting, convened three weeks after the first, the Central Asians plus Armenia, Azerbaijan and Moldova were admitted to the CIS (Georgia joined later and under some degree of Russian duress). This unplanned expansion effectively diluted the original vision of Yeltsin and his advisers. They had envisaged the CIS as being a geographically limited but economically, politically and even militarily significant union of Slavic states. As such, they might have been capable of dominating the former Soviet area.[64] In fact, the CIS in practice developed into a looser and broader arrangement, following the admission of the other republics.

There have been periodic attempts to inject new life into the expanded CIS, most of them at Russian instigation. During 1995 and 1996, for example, the possibility arose that the CIS, under Russian influence and leadership, might be remodelled as an eastern equivalent of the original European Economic Community, on the basis of the commercial and economic co-operation and integration being developed between Russia, Belarus, Kazakhstan and Kyrgyzstan.[65] Yet, the Yeltsin government subsequently backed away from specific suggestions of reintegration between Russia and Belarus, despite pressure from the latter's President. The Putin government has maintained this basic approach since 2000. This has led many analysts to the conclusion that Russian rhetorical support for measures of reintegration has essentially been a tactical device, with reintegration being threatened as, for example, a counter-measure to NATO's impending expansion into Central Europe and not viewed as an intrinsically beneficial process in its own right.[66] There has been little indication so far that Russian leaders have been prepared to seriously consider the pooling of national sovereignty that would be required if even a relatively limited EEC-type arrangement were to be created within the CIS area.[67]

Thus, it has remained unclear, in the Putin era, whether and to what extent attempts might be made to further develop the CIS. There have been periodic assertions by the President that improving relations with the other CIS states 'remains our indisputable priority in foreign policy'.[68] There were also reports during 2004 that Putin had instructed his National Security Council to devise a strategy designed to strengthen the CIS.[69] Yet, there has, so far, been little tangible sign of the CIS in the Putin era becoming a more significant and genuinely integrated international organisation than it was under Yeltsin.[70] Indeed, the series of upheavals in CIS states since 2003, beginning with the downfall of the Shevardnadze regime in Georgia and taking in the defeat of Viktor Yanukovich, Putin's favoured candidate, in the re-run presidential election in Ukraine in 2004 and the overthrow of President Askar Akayev in Kyrgyzstan in 2005, can all be seen as actually or potentially weakening Russian influence in these fellow CIS member states. President Shevardnadze had consented, albeit reluctantly, to the continued stationing of Russian 'peacekeeping' troops on Georgian territory and he had also taken Georgia into the CIS in 1993. In Ukraine, Yanukovich had opposed moves to prepare the country for eventual NATO membership. Akayev, finally, had consented to the establishing of a Russian military base in Kyrgyzstan, the first new Russian military installation outside the country's own territory since 1991.

Notwithstanding the points made above, there has been a lively debate amongst analysts and observers as to whether an underlying driver of Russian policy towards the other Soviet states has been a 'neo-imperialist impulse'. This debate was particularly pronounced during the 1990s. It was argued by some that Russian leaders' thinking was guided by 'a modified Brezhnev Doctrine'; that is, it was suggested that they viewed the sovereignty of near abroad states as being limited and they reserved the right to intervene militarily if they judged that vital Russian interests were under threat or at risk.[71] It was suggested by other analysts and observers, however, that those who detected a neo-imperialist agenda were ignoring 'the monumental role played by Yeltsin's government in destroying the Soviet empire' and the fact that 'the Yeltsin team voluntarily accepted the inviolability of borders between the newly independent nations, rejected [former Vice President] Rutskoi's appeals to mobilize Russians in the near abroad as Moscow's fifth column and instead demanded only that their basic human rights be observed'.[72] It has also been argued that the Russian political and military establishment has possessed neither the will nor the capability to intervene unilaterally or by force in other former Soviet republics.[73]

Overall, anybody who might have envisaged the CIS serving as an institutional tool for Russian domination of the former Soviet area has not had their expectations realised. This is not to say, on the other hand, that Russian policy towards the near abroad has become notice-ably softer during the course of the Putin presidency. On the contrary, the open political and diplomatic intervention in support of Viktor Yanukovich in Ukraine in November 2004 arguably surpassed any-thing attempted by Boris Yeltsin.[74] In addition, Russian policy towards the south western CIS states – chiefly Georgia and Moldova – has been censured, under Putin as under Yeltsin, for being primarily concerned with keeping them weak and divided by actively supporting ethnic separatists within them, as well as maintaining Russian military forces on their territory.[75]

Yet, as the years have progressed, there have been indications that the former Soviet republics have begun to consolidate their independ-ence. In 1995, Martha Brill Olcott concluded that, of the fourteen newly independent states apart from Russia, only the Baltic States, Ukraine, Turkmenistan, Uzbekistan and Azerbaijan were really com-mitted to full sovereignty and independence. Belarus, Kazakhstan, Kyrgyzstan and Tajikistan were, she argued, likely to be content with 'quasi-sovereignty'. In practical terms, this meant that these republics would rely on Russia to underpin their security and to provide economic support. Georgia, Moldova and Armenia were, in Olcott's view, undecided about which path to take.[76] Some at the time went even further than Olcott. Russian journalist and analyst Aleksander Tsipko argued that only the three Baltic States were fully committed to maintaining and consolidating their independence.[77]

It is doubtful whether any serious analyst would have made such claims a decade later. Since Olcott and Tsipko published their argu-ments, the Shevardnadze government in Georgia has, as noted, been replaced in 2003 by one widely seen as being more willing to assert Georgian sovereignty and less willing to do Russia's bidding. The autumn of 2004 saw the very public failure of the Russian govern-ment's intervention in support of Viktor Yanukovich as President of Ukraine. Election results in Moldova in March 2005 were also widely interpreted as an anti-Russian vote.[78]

In the Central Asian region, it has also been noted that the gov-ernment of Kazakhstan has been seeking to assert a role of regional leadership and putting forward its own proposals on possible future integration in the CIS, sometimes in competition with Russian ideas.[79] In Central Asia too, the United States has, since September 11 2001, established a military 'footprint' – that is to say, bases – in Kyrgyzstan and Uzbekistan. This presence, which was looking increasingly perma-nent as the 2000s progressed, may be helping to prompt a modification in Russian policy towards the near abroad region generally.

In the Yeltsin era, there were periodic assertions, from the President down, that the former Soviet area was, or should be, a sphere of exclusive Russian interest and influence. Thus, in a February 1993 statement for example, President Yeltsin called on the international community to give Russia 'special powers' as the 'guarantor of peace and stability' in 'the former USSR'. Yeltsin drew a parallel with the US. He stated that 'we recognise the specific role of the USA . . . in the regions of its vitally important interests, and expect the USA to take a similar approach towards the role of Russia on the basis of reciprocity'.[80] Since 2001, however, Putin has modified this line. In a July 2004 address to Russian diplomats, for example, he said that:

> We should not be hypnotized by declarations that nobody but Russia has the right to leadership over the CIS expanses. If we have recognised certain realities, these realities should be reckoned with and proceeded from in lining up our foreign policy. This approach . . . that no one except us has the right to work there is fundamentally wrong, lulling and disorienting.[81]

Putin's revised approach is almost certainly not to be taken as signalling a loss of interest in the near abroad on the part of the Russian leadership. Much more likely, it indicates pragmatic acceptance of the growing US presence and influence there, coupled with recognition that Russia, in future, will therefore have to compete for influence, rather than taking it as a given.[82] It is possible to see Putin's approach to the 2004 election in Ukraine in this light: active participation in a 'competition' between the 'pro-Russian' Yanukovich and the 'pro-western' Viktor Yushchenko. As suggested above, it would also be wrong to characterise Putin as being 'soft' in this area. On the contrary, by emphasising the possibility, even desirability, of competing with outside powers – chiefly the US – for influence and status, the Putin approach may actually increase the likelihood of future instances of Russian interference, as in Ukraine. Consequently, it may also increase the prospects for disputes over such meddling with the US and other western states.[83]

Russia and the Baltic States

The three Baltic States of Estonia, Latvia and Lithuania have, since 1991, been, in important respects, a special case in Russian foreign policy. They are the only former Soviet republics which have never been members of the CIS. During the 1990s, they were also the first ex-Soviet states to declare an interest in joining both NATO and the EU.

At the time of the Soviet break-up, there were some 25 million ethnic Russians and Russian speakers living outside Russia and in other states of the near abroad. Russian concerns about their treatment during the 1990s came to focus, in particular, on the Baltic republics of Estonia and Latvia. The possibility of eventual NATO enlargement to embrace the Baltic States was very likely one reason for this.[84] It was widely believed, in both Russia and amongst the NATO member states themselves, that the only former Soviet states with any real prospect of joining NATO in the medium term were the Baltic States. Although officially strongly opposed to this prospect, it is possible that Russian leaders also saw in it an opportunity. Respect for the rights of ethnic minorities within their borders was one of the general conditions laid down by NATO for those states aspiring to join its ranks.[85] Given the declared candidacies of all three Baltic States for NATO (and European Union)[86] membership, therefore, the Russian government had a source of potential leverage over both the Baltic governments and, indeed, NATO itself, in seeking redress for alleged infringements of the rights of Russians in the Baltic States.

Prominent amongst issues of contention have been citizenship and residency rights. In the early 1990s, official Russian concerns came to focus in particular on a draft Estonian 'Law on Aliens', which was intended to provide a legal basis for determining who would be permitted to reside in Estonia. Some Russian leaders asserted their concerns that the adoption of this law could lead to the mass expulsion of ethnic Russians living in that state. Regarding Latvia, meanwhile, Russian leaders objected, in particular, to proposals put forward during 1993 and 1994 to introduce annual quotas, limiting the numbers of ethnic Russians who could apply for Latvian citizenship.[87]

Western governments were aware that there were some genuine grounds for Russian concern. International institutions (though not NATO directly) were utilised extensively to try to find a means of addressing legitimate Russian concerns, whilst, at the same time, heading off any prospect of unilateral forcible Russian intervention in the Baltic region. From the early 1990s, UN fact-finding missions visited both Estonia and Latvia on several occasions. Both the Council of Europe (CoE) and the CSCE were also used to provide mechanisms through which proposed legislation by Estonia and Latvia on citizenship and residency could be subjected to international legal scrutiny, and suggestions made for improvements. An indication of the extent to which local ethnic Russians were feeling insecure at the time can be gauged from the fact that the first UN mission to Latvia in October 1992 reported having received over 300 petitions from ethnic Russians and other minority groups, complaining about 'arbitrary and discriminatory practices in the registration of Latvia's inhabitants'.[88]

Neither the UN nor the CSCE nor the CoE found evidence that ethnic Russians in the Baltic States were being systematically or seriously discriminated against by the governments of those states. On the other hand, the Balts' draft legislation was not always found to be wholly compatible with prevailing international norms and standards. During 1993, for example, it was reported that the President of Estonia had proposed twenty seven amendments to the draft Law on Aliens, based on recommendations made by the CSCE and the CoE.[89] Latvia's problems in trying to join the Council of Europe are also noteworthy in this context, in view of the fact that an important requirement for entry was the possession of citizenship laws which accorded with international norms. Lithuania and Estonia were both admitted to the CoE in 1993, whereas Latvian membership was delayed until 1995. Membership of the CoE mattered to the Baltic States, not only in its own right, but also because it was generally accepted as being an essential prerequisite for those seeking subsequently to join the EU and NATO.

Since the mid 1990s, public controversies over the status of Russians in the Baltic States have abated in both frequency and ferocity. Whilst not suggesting that all underlying problems have been resolved,[90] it appears that several factors have contributed to a gradual lessening of tensions.[91] Overall, the total number of Russians living in the Baltic States has steadily declined since the end of the Cold War. In 2001 it was reported that, based on census data, the Estonian Russian population had declined by 121,000 persons from 1989–99. In Latvia, meanwhile, the decline over the same period was 206,000 persons.[92]

There have been two main issues behind these headline figures. According to the report cited above, the chief contributory factors to the relative decline in the Russian populations have been 'assimilation' and 'migration loss in population exchange with Russia'. The former suggests that sections of the Russian communities in the Baltic States have become more effectively integrated into their wider societies, through, for example, inter-marriage with Estonians and Latvians as well as, in some cases, the formal granting of citizenship. In census returns, therefore, they were no longer counted as being 'Russian'. Even amongst the remaining non-citizens, there were indications of increasing willingness to, for example, engage in national political processes, and be accepted in doing so by the local indigenous populations.[93] On the Russian government's part, meanwhile, there was evidence of a move away from loud but largely rhetorical support for Russians in the near abroad and towards funding practical initiatives designed to, for example, promote the continued use of the Russian language in these states.[94]

The phrase 'migration loss in population exchange with Russia' was used to describe those Russians who emigrated from the Baltic States to Russia itself: reportedly 59,000 from Estonia and 94,000 from Latvia during the 1990s.[95] Inside Russia, important changes had been underway in terms of official attitudes to these influxes. In the early 1990s, the arrival of Russian migrants from other former Soviet republics had provoked concerns about the social and economic costs and consequences of integrating them into Russian society. It thus became a negative political issue. Even relatively moderate political figures, such as then Foreign Minister Andrei Kozyrev, publicly cited migration as 'the most palpable proof' of an 'unsatisfactory' attitude to ethnic Russian rights by the authorities in the other republics.[96] During the early years of the new century, such official attitudes began to change, largely as a result of Russia's own adverse demographic trends. Increasingly, migrant Russians (albeit of the 'right' type)[97] from near abroad states were to be welcomed for their potential contribution to mitigating the consequences of Russia's ongoing population decline.[98] Consequently, the migration issue showed clear signs of declining salience as an irritant in Russia–Baltic relations.

Perhaps the best indication of the extent to which the sting had been substantially drawn from Russia–Baltic relations can be seen by the official Russian reaction when the three Baltic States joined NATO and the EU in the spring of 2004. The muted response from the Russian government may have surprised some, given the verbose and public opposition to earlier rounds of NATO enlargement. It is true that there were major irritants between Russia and both NATO and the EU, as a result of this round of enlargement. However, these were the subject of negotiation between Russia and the institutions themselves and they did not arise directly out of the policies being pursued by Baltic governments. In NATO's case, the main issue was the question of the deployment of allied military forces and supporting infrastructure in the Baltic region. In the case of the EU, the most important and contentious debates were over transit rights for Russians travelling to and from Kaliningrad.

Conclusion

In many ways, Russia and NATO have both been very active since 1991 in responding to the challenges of adapting to the emerging post-Cold War international security environment. Yet, neither has so far managed to settle definitively the question of what its core nature should be or what roles it can and should aspire to play on the international stage, particularly with regard to Europe. Dean Acheson's famous 1960s quip about the United Kingdom – that it has lost an empire but not yet found a role – seems equally appropriate when applied to contemporary Russia. In NATO's case, despite being active across a substantially broader range of issue areas than during the Cold War, it is arguable that the member states have so far failed to define a core role, or roles, for their institution.

The sense of uncertainty and insecurity that this has produced, on both sides, has very likely complicated attempts to develop firm and settled relations between them. With this proposition in mind, the discussions in the chapters that follow explore in detail the various efforts that have, nevertheless, been made since 1991 to develop a solid and mutually beneficial Russia–NATO relationship.

3 Unfulfilled partnerships
Russia and NATO from 'honeymoon' to Kosovo

Introduction

The discussions in this chapter trace the evolution of the Russia–NATO relationship from 1991 through to 1998, when the Kosovo crisis began to move centre-stage. This crisis, often regarded as representing the most significant challenge to Russia–NATO relations to date, will be examined in the next chapter. The period under consideration here can usefully be divided into three distinct phases. This exercise will help to both illustrate and explore the complexities of the relationship. It will also help in developing and illuminating the underlying continuities and themes, which characterised Russia–NATO relations during this period.

Phase One: uncertain honeymoon

As noted in Chapter 1, the years 1991–3 have been described as a 'honeymoon' in relations between Russia and the West. During this time, President Boris Yeltsin and Foreign Minister Andrei Kozyrev were widely seen – and sometimes criticised by political opponents inside Russia, from the Eurasianist camp amongst others – to be making good relations with the US and Western Europe their top foreign policy priority.

In December 1991, even as the break-up of the Soviet Union was being finalised, Yeltsin chose to make relations with NATO the subject of his first significant foreign policy initiative as the head of the government of newly independent Russia. He dispatched a letter to the leaders of NATO governments, then meeting in Brussels, declaring that 'today we are raising the question of Russia's membership of NATO' as a 'long-term political aim'.[1] Viewed as a piece of political theatre, this initiative undoubtedly succeeded. It caught international attention and made headlines world-wide. At the time, however, nearly all NATO governments, and western and Russian analysts, were inclined to downplay the seriousness of any official Russian intent to actually join NATO. The practical issues that this would raise seemed, almost instinctively, too overwhelming.[2] In any event, membership enlargement was not on the NATO agenda during 1991 and 1992, despite growing interest amongst leaders in Central Europe.

No considered or specific western response was, therefore, given to what was thought to be the purely hypothetical question of whether Russia could ever be envisaged as a NATO member. In retrospect, this apparent stand-offishness may be seen to have had negative consequences.[3] At the time, however, and to be fair to the NATO side, there did not seem to be any urgent need to seriously address the issue of possible Russian accession, given uncertainties over how and even whether Russian foreign policy was eventually going to 'settle down'. The Russian government itself did not follow up the initial Yeltsin letter in any clear way, although possibly this was because it was waiting for and expecting NATO to make the next move.

Western officials, for their part, recalled the context in which the letter had been sent. It arrived at NATO Headquarters during the first ministerial meeting of the institution's new North Atlantic Co-operation Council (NACC), a forum grouping NATO members with the non-Soviet members of the former Warsaw Pact and the three Baltic States, whose independence NATO governments had, by then, officially recognised. The NACC was to be the forerunner of the Partnership for Peace scheme and thus represented the formal beginning of NATO's external adaptation, a process discussed in Chapter 2. The main practical purpose of the Yeltsin letter seemed to have been to ensure that Russia was invited to participate in this new forum, as was duly agreed. That having been done, it was generally assumed within NATO that the Russians would be satisfied and, initially, the Russian side gave little indication to the contrary. The ensuing debate inside Russia on the prospects and desirability of its actually joining NATO remained low key and desultory.[4]

Despite the prevailing honeymoon atmosphere, certain underlying tensions still lingered. In December 1991, the new Russian State had taken over the Soviet foreign policy apparatus, with most of its staffers and officials. An in-built suspicion of NATO, and especially any potential move east by the institution, characterised the attitudes of much of this *apparat*. These institutionalised influences were visible even in early statements by the relatively liberal Russian Foreign Minister. In February 1993, for example, Kozyrev wrote that Russia was:

Opposed to closed groupings, to doctrines such as Pax Americana, Pax Germanica or Pax Eurasiatica. A present-day balance of forces and equilibrium in the interests of states can be achieved only in a 'common space' where everyone is interdependent and helps one another; if there are disputes, these will be settled within a legal framework.[5]

Other senior Russians were showing signs of sensitivity about NATO developing engagement programmes with countries in their 'strategic corset' region – the 'near abroad'. There existed, in some quarters, an evident belief that NATO members intended to disrupt the nascent CIS. In December 1992, for example, Marshal Yevgeny Shaposhnikov, Commander of the Joint Armed Forces of the CIS States, claimed that 'when NATO spoke about a closer cooperation with some of the countries of the CIS they did it, either intentionally or unintentionally, to encourage the disintegration processes within the Commonwealth'.[6]

Thus, even at the height of the Russia–NATO honeymoon, there was an undercurrent of tension. During 1992 and the first half of 1993, the underlying tension remained largely latent. The NATO engagement programmes set in train under the auspices of the NACC remained limited and focused on seminars and meetings, rather than anything more operational. As long as NACC activities remained at this relatively low level, it was difficult to conceive of them as posing any real threat to the integrity of the CIS or of Russia itself. Most importantly, the question of possible membership enlargement into Central Europe was not yet officially on the NATO agenda.

In the summer of 1993, however, the enlargement issue suddenly broke open. Ironically, the debate was initiated – albeit almost certainly unintentionally – by President Yeltsin himself. On an official visit to Poland in late August, he agreed to a joint declaration with the then Polish President, Lech Walesa, which included the statement that:

The presidents touched on the matter of Poland's intention to join NATO. President L. Walesa set forth Poland's well-known position on this count, which was met with understanding by President B. N. Yeltsin. *In the long term, such a decision taken by a sovereign Poland in the interests of overall European integration does not go against the interests of other states, including the interests of Russia* [emphasis added].[7]

Yeltsin's apparent endorsement of Polish aspirations to join NATO (repeated, in the case of the Czech Republic, on a visit to Prague, immediately following his Polish tour) was instrumental in transforming the political landscape. Hitherto, outside of Central Europe, the debate, in so far as it had existed, had been conducted largely amongst analysts and think-tanks, with little obvious impact on policy makers. After August 1993, however, enlargement was to become increasingly the dominant theme in the whole Russia–NATO relationship.

It is, therefore, of prime importance to try to establish why Yeltsin signed up to this Warsaw Declaration. Some argued that it was a classic case of him 'freelancing'.[8] Perhaps the President was seeking to assert himself politically, by taking a dramatic, and seemingly decisive, policy initiative in contradiction to the line laid out by his own foreign minister on the eve of the Polish visit.[9] It is also possible that the Russian leadership simply underestimated the potential of the enlargement debate to escalate and move centre-stage as rapidly as it subsequently did. There had been relatively little public debate on NATO enlargement inside Russia following Yeltsin's initial letter of December 1991, suggesting, perhaps, that Russian leaders, officials and public opinion had not considered it a serious issue. The phrase 'the presidents touched on the matter of Poland's intention to join NATO' in the Warsaw Declaration suggested that it had not been a dominant theme of their discussions. Perhaps, then, the Russians had simply failed to engage adequately with the implications of possible NATO enlargement into Central Europe, and Yeltsin and his aides had not formed a firm position one way or the other before Walesa confronted him with the issue in Warsaw.[10]

It is crucial to note the significance of the exact wording of the agreed text, particularly the statement that Polish accession to NATO 'in the interests of overall European integration' would not threaten Russia's interests. The Russian Foreign Ministry subsequently bemoaned the frequency with which western officials and commentators chose to overlook this qualification when suggesting that Russia had simply assented to NATO enlargement, with no strings attached. In a commentary published in *Segodnya* in early September 1993, foreign ministry official Vyacheslav Yelagin set out the ministry's basic line. This was, first, one opposing the *rapid* enlargement of NATO membership, whilst recognising that former Warsaw Pact states had the right to join, if they so chose. Second, according to Yelagin, the foreign ministry's preference was for 'strengthening and improving such structures as CSCE and the North Atlantic Cooperation Council'; that is, institutions and structures within which Russia had a seat.

Finally, implicit in Yelagin's argument was that Russia – as a great power or even a continuing superpower as some were suggesting at the time – should develop a 'special relationship' with NATO, *before* any enlargement into Central Europe was considered.[11]

In mid September, President Yeltsin addressed a letter to the US, FRG, France and the UK, setting out similar views on the future of European security. This clearly suggested, therefore, that the views contained within the letter now constituted Russia's official stance on the subject of NATO enlargement. The Yeltsin letter was widely perceived at the time as an attempt to walk back from his apparent endorsement of enlargement in Warsaw. The main source of pressure was generally assumed to be coming from the Russian armed forces: 'the greatest hindrance to Russia's closer relationship with NATO'.[12] In this context, it is important to remember the political turmoil in Russia in September and October 1993, namely a constitutional crisis and consequent armed stand-off between Yeltsin and members of the federal parliament, which was eventually 'resolved' by the application of military force. It was, therefore, assumed that the perceived hardening of the President's line on NATO enlargement was a direct result of the debt he owed to the Russian military for saving his political career at this chaotic time.[13]

Yeltsin's letter to President Bill Clinton *et al.* was clear in its core message: 'security must be indivisible and must rest on pan-European structures'. Otherwise, he asserted, there was a risk of 'neo-isolation of [Russia] as opposed to its natural introduction into the Euro-Atlantic space'. There was also evidence of an acknowledgement of pressures at home. The letter cited the potential impact of NATO enlargement into Central Europe on Russian public opinion, 'not only the opposition, but the moderates, too'. He was also somewhat vaguer about the prospect of eventual Russian accession to NATO – calling it 'a theoretical proposition' – than in his original December 1991 communication.[14]

Those who believe that the influence of the armed forces was an important factor at this time can point to the military doctrine, which the Russian government adopted in November 1993. The leaked text, reportedly drafted substantially by the armed forces themselves, identified 'the expansion of military blocs and alliances to the detriment of the interests of the Russian Federation's military security' as being amongst 'the basic existing and potential sources of military danger' to Russia.[15]

There is also some evidence of a sense of disappointment amongst Russians in the political leadership that Yeltsin's original December 1991 signal had not, as they saw it, been picked up and acted upon by NATO. Some, it seems, had taken the idea of eventual Russian membership seriously. In October 1993, Sergei Karaganov, a member of Yeltsin's Presidential Council, suggested that:

> These [Central European] countries have absolute right [*sic*] to get into whatever alliance they want, however from the Russian perspective that means a strengthening of a nation's opposition here and also geopolitical isolation of the country, so what we are offering – why not Russia [*sic*]. Russia has asked for membership two years ago.[16]

Yeltsin himself, perhaps mindful of the possible response from opponents at home, did not go this far in his letter to western leaders, as noted.[17] Nevertheless, he did indicate that he had expected a better response from NATO. As he put it:

> We favor a situation where the relations between our country and NATO would be by several degrees warmer than those between the Alliance and Eastern Europe. NATO–Russia rapprochement, including through their interaction in the peace-making arena, should proceed on a faster track. The East Europeans, too, could be involved in this process.[18]

NATO leaders could not have asked for a clearer statement of what the President wanted: a special relationship that elevated Russia above NATO's other eastern interlocutors and so recognised its status as a great power. This arrangement would also recognise – in Russian eyes – their country's status as a predominantly (and predominant) European power. The perceived reluctance of NATO members to adequately address this demand at their January 1994 Brussels summit meeting was to play a major role in provoking the deterioration in relations that subsequently ensued.

During the remaining months of 1993, the Russian government, despite its domestic travails, managed to maintain its basic position on the future of NATO and European security. This was formally and most clearly expressed in an 'open report' published by the Foreign Intelligence Service (FIS), then headed by Yevgeny Primakov, in November. The FIS report seemed like an attempt to establish a composite stance, which could embrace both the armed forces and mainstream political leaders. Primakov took care to stress that his report had the endorsement of military leaders[19] and, although he denied that he had also cleared it with the President and foreign ministry before publication, it was widely suspected that he had, in fact, done so.[20]

The FIS report introduced and developed the theme that Russia should oppose the enlargement of NATO's membership, if such a move were made in isolation. If, on the other hand, membership enlargement were part of a fundamental reform of the institution's purposes, roles and structures, the Russian response could be different. The report was not, therefore, opposed to NATO enlargement under all circumstances. It concluded that:

> It would be in Russia's interests if the process of expanding the zone of NATO's responsibility were synchronized with a change in the nature of that alliance and with an adaptation of its functions to the special features of the present stage of historical development.[21]

Phase Two: deterioration and revival

The first attempt at partnership

In autumn 1993, NATO members had accepted an American suggestion for what became the Partnership for Peace initiative and this was subsequently adopted at the Brussels summit. PfP is an umbrella term that covers military contact and co-operation activities between NATO members and non-members in Europe. It embraces both a discursive element, on issues such as democratic control of armed forces, and joint military training and exercise programmes. Not the least important, it also gives interested eastern partners an opportunity to become involved in a multinational force-planning process closely modelled on NATO's own.[22]

The initial response to PfP from the Yeltsin government had been positive.[23] It was clear from the beginning, however, that this response was conditioned, in the minds of Russian leaders, on the partnership scheme being an *alternative* to NATO enlargement.[24] At the time, NATO members appear to have played up to this. At the NATO Foreign Ministers meeting in December 1993, support was specifically expressed for Yeltsin and his policies and no reference was made to enlargement. The media spin, at least, seemed to be deliberately designed to damp down any expectations that a NATO enlargement process was in the offing. The then German Chancellor, Helmut Kohl, was quoted as saying that 'we have great understanding for the security needs of . . . our East European neighbours, but we see no chance of them joining NATO'.[25] It was also reported that, at the NATO meeting, 'there was unanimity that a comprehensive security partnership with Russia should come first, and only then could there be any question of expanding Nato's own ranks'.[26] This was undoubtedly what Yeltsin, Kozyrev and Primakov wanted to hear.

The favourable mood – from a Russian perspective – continued up to and during the Brussels summit, despite the fact that the resulting declaration seemed to open the door, at some point in the future, to NATO enlargement.[27] This seemed to many, and not just in Russia, to be little more than diplomatic window dressing, designed to keep Central European states on board to the extent of persuading them to sign up for PfP.

Yet, there was a sense of foreboding, even at this time. Initially, this was concerned not with enlargement, as much as the possibly undesirable consequences of PfP as it developed. It was, perhaps, not too surprising to hear a senior Russian military officer state that 'Partnership for Peace is a program for establishing strategic influence in Eastern Europe and moving NATO's forward lines right up to Russia's western borders.' The upper echelons of the armed forces may also have been worried that the military transparency implicit in PfP might shed light on practices and activities within the Russian military establishment that they would prefer to keep from public view. On the other hand, no less a supposed dove than Mikhail Gorbachev wrote after the Brussels summit: 'let's call a spade a spade, Partnership for Peace means that the NATO infrastructure would gradually draw closer to Russia's borders . . . with all the ensuing consequences; joint military maneuvers and movements of NATO armed forces in direct proximity to Russia's borders'.[28]

These sentiments reflected one of the main sources of Russian disenchantment with NATO that became evident during 1994. This was a belief that Russia had been duped about the true nature and aims of PfP. During the months following the Brussels summit, a debate was kindled amongst Russian parliamentarians, analysts and commentators about the desirability of the country signing up for PfP. Strong views were expressed against it. Vladimir Lukin, the Chairman of the Russian *Duma*'s International Affairs Committee, in a striking metaphor much quoted in the western media, compared PfP to 'the propositions made by a rapist who has cornered a girl: she can either resist or submit, but the result will be the same'.[29]

Lukin and other prominent Russian policy makers were reportedly concerned that PfP, which NATO had declared to be open to all the ex-Soviet and ex-Warsaw Pact states, was deliberately designed to disrupt and undermine the CIS. This was not a new concern, as noted, but it did receive a new lease of life.[30] Another key concern was that

PfP was designed as a covert route to eventual NATO enlargement. In fact, a link had been *openly* made in the Brussels summit declarations. Here it was stated that 'active participation in the Partnership for Peace will play an important role in the evolutionary process of the expansion of NATO'.[31] Some Russian leaders concluded that it made little sense for Russia itself to become involved in an initiative that was thus linked to NATO enlargement.

A crisp summary of the major concerns of the opponents of Russian participation was provided by political scientist Vladislav Chernov in *Nezavisimaya Gazeta* in February 1994. In addition to the potential impact on the CIS, Chernov itemised the concerns thus:

- that the PfP's 'motive force' was made up 'primarily of the anti-Russia sentiments of our former friends'; a perception that was exacerbated by statements from leaders in Central Europe suggesting that Russia was still regarded as a security threat;
- that PfP was a subterfuge designed to 'ensure a US military presence in Poland and Hungary';
- that, given a focus within PfP on bringing Central and Eastern European armed forces up to NATO standards, the programme would work to the detriment of Russian arms manufacturers who had traditionally dominated the market in these regions.[32]

Against the domestic opposition, the Russian Foreign Ministry was the leading proponent of joining PfP at this time. It deployed two main arguments. First, that PfP was an important element in the transformation of NATO from a Cold War military bloc, which is what the previous year's FIS report had stated Russia wanted. In March 1994, Andrei Kozyrev asserted that:

> The virtue and, if you want it, farsightedness of the Partnership for Peace program adopted by the NATO leaders is that ... as it opens up NATO, [it] makes the first step towards transforming it from a bloc into some other form of organizing security. Therefore, it fully complies with our concept of all-European partnership. In the future we may also see the opening of a communications channel between the CIS and NATO.[33]

The Russian Foreign Ministry's second argument was that non-participation would leave Russia isolated. First Deputy Foreign Minister Vitaly Churkin claimed that underlying the domestic debates was 'a serious ideological confrontation between proponents and opponents of Russian isolationism'. He added that 'I am convinced that a path of isolation from the world community holds no promise' [for Russia].[34]

By the early spring of 1994, it appeared as if the proponents of Russia joining the Partnership for Peace were gaining the upper hand. At the beginning of March, a diplomatic signal to the effect that Russia was preparing to come aboard was reportedly received at NATO Headquarters in Brussels.[35] That it did not subsequently do so at this time was due principally to the impact within Russian policy-making circles of the threat and use of NATO airstrikes against Serb forces in Bosnia. This occasioned what one analyst has called 'the first significant crisis in relations between the West and Russia after the end of the Cold War'.[36]

Although NATO had formally stood ready to use airpower in supp-ort of United Nations' relief and protection efforts in Bosnia since the previous summer, its first serious threat to do so was not made until February 1994. The first actual airstrikes took place three months later, at almost the exact time that had been pencilled in for a PfP signing visit by the Russian Foreign Minister to NATO Headquarters. In February, Russia had intervened to broker a deal with the Bosnian Serbs, which had prevented the threatened NATO strikes from actu-ally being carried out. This move had been greeted by some as the first significant sign that post-Cold War Russia was able and willing to put together and assert a distinct stance on an important issue, directly influencing the policy of NATO members as a result. Russia, *Izvestia* exulted, 'with one step put itself at the center of attention. It was at that moment that Russia found the important place that it alone can occupy and played the role that no one else could have played. Bravo!'[37] One western analyst, in similar vein, argued that the Russians were able to use this situation 'as a means to reintroduce themselves as a great power on the world stage'.[38]

Thus, for many Russians, something far more important than the future of Bosnia itself was perceived to be at stake: nothing less than their country's status as a great power, particularly in the European context, and its right to be respected as such. It is, therefore, easy to understand why the actual use of airpower by NATO in April 1994 – with no prior consultation with the Russian government – generated a particularly hostile backlash. It was, indeed, the stated reason for postponing Russia's accession to the PfP.

However, it is important to stress that the decision was for a post-ponement, not a cancellation. The use of airpower in Bosnia did not induce Russia – or at least the Russian Foreign Ministry – to scrap all efforts at co-operating with NATO. Rather, the emphasis was changed. In explaining the postponement decision, Kozyrev stated that 'we are interested in much more serious relations with NATO than a mere framework document, so that surprises and unilateral measures, especially military ones, can be ruled out in those zones where we must cooperate very closely'.[39] What this statement portended was that the foreign ministry was about to renew the demand that Russia's status as a great power entitled it to a special relationship – and most especially privileged consultation rights – with NATO.[40] As Vladimir Baranovsky later put it, the Russian government had decided that 'being equal [was] as unacceptable as being isolated'.[41]

Evidently anxious not to see the legitimacy of its new partnership scheme being undermined by indefinite Russian non-participation, NATO signalled a willingness, in principle, to discuss special arrangements.[42] Thus, from April 1994, attention, both in Russia and at NATO, was focused increasingly on the Russian demand for a privileged relationship with NATO.

Two months later, following a half-yearly NATO Foreign Ministers meeting, an important diplomatic signal was sent to Moscow in the final communiqué:

> We reaffirm our strong support for political and economic reform in Russia and recognize the important contributions to European stability and security that Russia can make on a wide range of issues. Accordingly, we wish to develop constructive relations of mutual respect, benefit and friendship between Russia and the Alliance . . . We hope and expect that Russia will also join us in developing an extensive and far-reaching Individual Partnership Programme, corresponding to its size, importance, capabilities, and willingness to contribute to the pursuit of shared objectives. As with all Partners, our relationship with Russia, *including in appropriate areas outside the Partnership for Peace*, will be developed over time [emphasis added].[43]

This statement contained a key concession from NATO, as emphasised. Hitherto, NATO members had always insisted that no special side deals were possible with individual partners over and above the PfP. Rather, they argued, there was sufficient flexibility built into the PfP to satisfy all the eastern participants. In June 1994, they accepted a breach in this principle, in order to finally persuade the Russian government to sign up.

The details and substance of the prospective Russia–NATO special relationship were supposed to be filled in subsequently. It was intended, as the NATO statement suggested, that this would happen as Russia also developed its Individual Partnership Programme within PfP. Areas of potential future co-operation were sketched out in a 'Summary of Conclusions' of discussions between NATO members and Foreign Minister Kozyrev in Brussels.[44] This was issued at the same time as Kozyrev finally signed Russia up for PfP in principle[45] on 22 June 1994.[46]

The informal basis of the deal was a formula which came to be known as 'no vetoes, no surprises'. Under this, the Russians accepted that new consultative arrangements would *not* accord them the status of full participants, with veto rights, in NATO decision making. In return, Kozyrev asked for, and NATO members agreed, that the latter would not make major decisions without consulting Russia first. As an apparent gesture of good faith, the five leading NATO members (the US, FRG, France, the UK and Italy) agreed to convene an informal 'Contact Group', specifically to discuss Bosnian issues, with Russia as the sixth participant.[47] What the Russian government had uppermost in its mind when pressing for 'no surprises' was a desire to ensure that it would have plenty of warning should NATO members ever decide to seriously proceed with an enlargement process. This was made clear by Kozyrev at the press conference that followed his PfP signing ceremony.[48]

By the middle of 1994, it appeared as if the deterioration in Russia–NATO relations, which had occurred in the first half of the year, had been arrested and, further, that the prospects for its reversal were promising. Both the NATO and Russian sides had committed themselves to developing a special relationship, that is, one that went beyond what was available to NATO's other eastern partners through PfP. They pledged to work out the details and meet again at the next round of NATO ministerial meetings at the end of the year.

In December, however, things went awry. Andrei Kozyrev, who had been due to meet his NATO partners to set the seal on the detail of the new links and programmes, pulled out at the last minute. He objected to the inclusion in the communiqué issued at the meeting of NATO Foreign Ministers, which had just taken place, of a commitment to 'initiate a process of examination inside the Alliance to determine how NATO will enlarge, the principles to guide this process and the implications of membership'.[49] This, argued Kozyrev, violated the principle of 'no surprises', as Russia had not been forewarned about it. Unconvinced by NATO protestations that what had been set in train was a technical study process without any wider implications, Kozyrev stated that a 'hasty and unwarranted expansion of the alliance is not to

Russia's liking'.[50] The new chill in relations appeared confirmed when, five days later, President Yeltsin gave his 'cold peace' speech to the CSCE summit in Budapest, as noted in Chapter 1.

To some observers, these developments represented a watershed. Looking back four years later, Russian analyst Igor Maksimychev saw 1994 in these terms, due to 'the turn made by the West . . . from common European solutions to the attempts to make Smaller Europe [that is, NATO] the continent's leader'.[51] But was the December NATO decision really such a surprise?

During the course of 1994, the position of the Clinton administration on NATO enlargement had undergone significant development. At the beginning of the year, the US had been content to ensure that a rhetorical statement in favour of eventual enlargement was endorsed at the Brussels summit. Immediately thereafter, President Clinton had journeyed to Prague to meet the leaders of the Czech Republic, Hungary and Poland. His remarks on enlargement at that time seemed designed to damp down any expectations that the Brussels statement would presage a rapid opening of NATO's doors. Clinton warned Central European leaders against pressing for 'immediate membership' and risking the drawing of a 'new line in Europe' between themselves and states to their east, which could not or would not join. His remarks also implicitly linked future NATO enlargement to the success or failure of the Russian political and economic reform process and he urged his listeners 'not to assume the failure of Russia's reforms' by pressing intently for early NATO membership.[52]

By the summer of 1994, this position had shifted markedly. This became apparent in remarks made by Clinton and then Secretary of State Warren Christopher during a visit to Poland. In an address to the Polish Parliament in July, the President stated that NATO enlargement would 'not depend upon the appearance of a new threat in Europe'.[53] Christopher, meanwhile, said that NATO member governments 'should discuss among themselves what the next step should be' in the enlargement process.[54] This was the genesis of the NATO decision to initiate the enlargement study process, which so annoyed Andrei Kozyrev in December 1994.

The decoupling of NATO enlargement from the external security environment, which these remarks presaged, was a significant departure from the US position that Clinton had put forward in Prague seven months previously. Now it was clear that enlargement was desired by the administration for reasons not wholly, or even mainly, dependent on the course of Russian reform. Some have argued that this change was motivated mainly by domestic concerns and that Clinton was thinking about forthcoming midterm congressional elections and the potential influence of voters of Central European descent. Elsewhere, the present author has developed the argument that events in the European Union's own evolving enlargement process were more influential.[55]

Why did the US and its NATO allies not make greater efforts to bring the Russians on board during the months leading up to the December ministerial meeting, so as to eliminate the risk of the latter's leaders being unacceptably 'surprised'? Arguably, an attempt to do so was in fact made. On his first trip to Europe in January 1994, President Clinton had journeyed to Moscow for a summit with Boris Yeltsin. During a question-and-answer session in the course of this visit, Clinton was asked about US views of Russian military activity in the CIS area. In his reply, he stated that 'you will be more likely to be involved in some of these areas near you, just like the United States has been involved in the last several years in Panama and Grenada near our area'.[56]

This seemed to some to be a *de facto* signal by Clinton of US willingness to tacitly recognise and hence condone the development of a Russian sphere of influence over the states of the near abroad. Former National Security Advisor Zbigniew Brzezinski, for example, accused the Clinton administration of effectively giving the Russians *carte blanche* for military intervention in the near abroad, thus limiting the sovereignty of the former Soviet republics.[57]

In September 1994, the US press reported the leak of what was allegedly a 'State Department policy paper circulating in high diplomatic circles'. According to the reports, this paper 'understood that a Russian sphere of influence is being recognized with Europe extending to the eastern border of Poland, leaving the Baltics somewhat up for grabs'.[58] Although the State Department denied that any such document existed, allegations that a carve-up of Europe had, in effect, been agreed by the US and Russia persisted through that autumn. They were reinforced by President Yeltsin's forceful claim to Russian 'special interests' in the CIS region, which he asserted at the UN General Assembly.[59] There was also press speculation – in both the United States and Russia – that Russian support for a UN Security Council Resolution authorising a US-led intervention in Haiti had been bought at the price of US recognition of a Russian sphere of influence in the near abroad.[60]

The sweeping victory of the Republican Party in the US congressional elections in November 1994 effectively put paid to any emerging understandings. The Republican leadership had made clear its disquiet about the Clinton administration's 'Russia First' policy, especially the alleged extent to which the President had over-personalised his relationship with his Russian counterpart. In his newly diminished state, President Clinton opted not to pick a fight. The line was formally drawn in his speech to the CSCE summit in Budapest in December. As well as asserting that no outsider (that is, Russia) would be able to veto NATO enlargement, Clinton also called for the CSCE to 'guard against the assertion of hegemony or spheres of influence' within its area.[61]

It can, therefore, reasonably be speculated that the apparently abrupt deterioration in Russia–NATO relations in December 1994 owed much to the breakdown of the attempt to put together an informal 'grand bargain'. Russian acquiescence in NATO enlargement into Central Europe would have been traded for US recognition of Russian primacy in the CIS area. However, that deal had now been derailed.

On top of this, the extent to which Russian leaders were displeased by what they perceived to be NATO's gratuitous decision to speed up the enlargement process in December 1994 should not be underestimated. Their main concern during the first part of 1995 was a desire to halt the perceived 'rush'. This was a core theme in virtually all the public statements made by Russian leaders at the time. In March, for example, President Yeltsin stated that 'we are against a sudden, accelerated, large-scale expansion of NATO', whilst Foreign Minister Kozyrev asked rhetorically 'why rush things?'[62] In April, Defence Minister General Pavel Grachev threatened that Russia would abandon key arms control and disarmament agreements if NATO continued its 'rush to expand to the east'.[63] Arguing in a somewhat more measured manner, Alexei Arbatov wrote that, in order to 'limit the damage' which enlargement would cause to relations between Russia and the West, 'the first step is to make this process as slow and gradual as possible'. Arbatov recommended 'including the Central European states one by one at decent intervals, for the governments and public to avoid shocks and have time to adopt [*sic*] to the new environment'.[64]

Despite their growing differences, the late spring of 1995 offered an unusual opportunity for the main players to try to reach another compromise. Early May saw the fiftieth anniversary of the end of the Second World War in Europe. It was announced that President Clinton would be coming to Europe for a summit meeting with President Yeltsin in Moscow.

Immediately prior to this visit, the US floated a new formula as the basis for Russia–NATO relations. In a speech in London at the beginning of May, the then US Ambassador to NATO, Robert Hunter, stated that 'at NATO, we are ready to give Russia a voice, but not a veto over Alliance decisions'.[65] This represented not only a reformulation, but also an enhancement, of the old 'no vetoes, no surprises' concept. The Russians were now being promised both greater and more embedded consultation rights with NATO and its member states.

The new proposal helped to ensure that a major row over enlargement was avoided at the Yeltsin–Clinton meeting in Moscow. More concretely, it helped to pave the way, finally, for the Russian government to agree to complete its PfP Individual Partnership Programme. This it did at a meeting of NATO foreign ministers in the Netherlands at the end of May. With this decision, Russia thus acceded fully to the Partnership for Peace programme. Despite there having been plenty of rhetoric on all sides about the desirability of establishing a partnership, it had taken nearly eighteen months for Russia's accession to NATO's existing partnership programme to be fully effected.

Moving forward?

At the May 1995 Russia–NATO gathering, 'Areas for Pursuance of a Broad, Enhanced NATO/Russia Dialogue and Co-operation' were also agreed. These included, most significantly, provision for ' "16+1" discussions in the North Atlantic Council, Political Committee or other appropriate Alliance fora', bringing together Russian representatives and those from the then sixteen NATO member states.[66] This new standing (as opposed to *ad hoc*) consultative arrangement went beyond anything offered to any other non-NATO member state. By early 1997, the 16+1 consultative format had reportedly been used on 'two dozen' occasions.[67] There can be little doubt that the existence of the 16+1 consultations did help to draw some of the sting from the enlargement issue as a source of disturbance to Russia–NATO relations from mid 1995.

Another key factor was the *de facto* decision by NATO members not to proceed with enlargement until after the Russian parliamentary and presidential elections, scheduled for December 1995 and June 1996 respectively. Amongst other tactics, the Russian diplomatic establishment had utilised a somewhat unusual public tool in order to press for this. It took the form of a newspaper article in the name of Anatoly Adamishin, the Russian Ambassador to the UK, which was timed to coincide with the NATO meeting in the Netherlands. This article, published in the now-defunct newspaper *The European*, called on NATO members 'to announce a moratorium on the expansion of Nato – let's say for the whole of next year' [that is, 1996].[68] The NATO members were not prepared to go quite that far and no public announcements on a moratorium were made. However, private assurances had been given to Russian leaders in advance of the NATO meeting.[69]

The extent to which the moves made in the late spring and early summer of 1995 helped to mend fences may be gauged from the fact that the publication, in September, of the *Study on NATO Enlargement* passed largely without comment in Russia. Nor, in keeping with the *de facto* moratorium, did it result in any obvious or short-term action by NATO members. Following the negotiation of the Dayton peace accords for Bosnia in the autumn of 1995, and the subsequent deployment of a multinational NATO-led peace Implementation Force (IFOR), Russian troops began working with their NATO counterparts on the ground there. This had two benefits. First, it demonstrated that practical co-operation between Russia and NATO was possible. Second, it gave additional impetus to the formalised links, including the 16+1 format, which were beginning to develop following the May 1995 agreement.

By the beginning of 1996, there were new faces at the helm at both NATO Headquarters and in the Russian Foreign Ministry. At NATO, Secretary-General Willy Claes resigned after a corruption scandal and was replaced by former Spanish Foreign Minister, Javier Solana. In Russia, meanwhile, Andrei Kozyrev had been sacked, in part as a result of what President Yeltsin had seen as a premature attempt to define the terms under which Russia could accept eventual NATO enlargement.[70] His replacement was Yevgeny Primakov, author of the 1993 FIS report on enlargement and Russian interests.

Primakov was sometimes referred to in the western media as a foreign policy hawk, seen as an unbending opponent of NATO enlargement under any circumstances.[71] It should have been remembered, however, that his FIS report had not ruled out enlargement *per se*. He had argued that it *could* be acceptable, providing that it was but one part of a fundamental transformation of NATO. This suggested pragmatism and flexibility. Such an impression was confirmed during the course of 1996 when, using NATO's *de facto* enlargement moratorium to good effect, Primakov indicated the conditions under which enlargement into Central Europe might be acceptable.

Primakov's conditions (ironically, similar to those reportedly formulated by Kozyrev and which had helped to get him sacked) related to the modalities of enlargement. The Russian demands were, first, that no nuclear weapons or supporting infrastructure should be stationed on the territory of new members. Second, the eastward movement of NATO military infrastructure *per se* should be kept to a minimum or preferably not happen at all. It was also reported that the Russian government sought agreement by NATO members to rule out an enlargement embracing the Baltic States or any other former Soviet countries.[72]

In addition to considering these conditions, the United States made a move in the late summer of 1996 on the issue of further upgrading NATO's institutional relations with the Russians. In early September, Secretary of State Christopher delivered a major speech on the future of European security in the FRG. During this speech, he flagged up the end of the *de facto* moratorium on NATO enlargement, now that the Russian elections were over. He announced a NATO summit for summer 1997 and asserted that this would be the occasion to issue invitations to the first Central European candidates to begin accession negotiations. Simultaneously, however, he declared that, in future:

> Russia's cooperation with NATO should be expressed in a formal charter. This charter should create standing arrangements for consultation and joint action between Russia and the alliance . . . The charter we seek should give us a permanent mechanism for crisis management so we can respond together immediately as . . . challenges arise.[73]

This was a major public opening. The Russian government had long pressed for its relationship with NATO to be formalised in a binding document. It would have preferred one that was legally binding, but would accept one that was viewed by both sides as being politically binding. Hitherto, NATO member states had resisted this and had restricted the relationship, outside PfP, to the level of declaratory statements.

In autumn 1996, the Clinton administration began gearing up for the NATO ministerial meetings at the end of the year, at which it expected the basic elements of Christopher's concept – enlargement plus enhanced relations with Russia – to be formally adopted. The task of publicly selling the proposed Russia–NATO charter evidently fell mainly to the then Defense Secretary, William Perry. Perry was rhetorically effusive. Speaking in Moscow in October, for example, he declared that:

> [W]e must create a new, enhanced role for Russia within NATO, a role in which Russia should be able to participate in most of the activities of NATO . . . [W]e would welcome and hope that Russia

would play a major role in a superpartnership commensurate with its status as a great power.[74]

At the December meeting of NATO Foreign Ministers, it was confirmed that a summit would be held in the summer of 1997 to, among other things, invite 'one or more' states to join. Concessions were offered to the Russians too. NATO members had devised what came to be known as the 'three nos' formula. This addressed the thorny issue of nuclear weapons specifically and pledged that:

> Enlarging the Alliance will not require a change in NATO's current nuclear posture and therefore, NATO countries have no intention, no plan, and no reason to deploy nuclear weapons on the territory of new members nor any need to change any aspect of NATO's nuclear posture or nuclear policy – and we do not foresee any future need to do so.[75]

Realistically, this political (but not legally binding) commitment was as far as NATO members could go without conceding a Russian veto over their future nuclear posture.

On the issue of further enhancements to the Russia–NATO institutional relationship, the December 1996 communiqué confirmed the US proposal that this 'could take the form of a Charter'. The more grandiose American ideas for Russian 'political membership' of NATO were absent, however, reflecting the caution of its European members. Instead, the direction of the statement was towards an evolutionary development of the existing 16+1 consultations, supplemented by more 'military liaison and co-operation', building upon that which had developed through co-operation in IFOR in Bosnia. The NATO members also announced that the task of negotiating the charter would be entrusted to Secretary-General Solana. This was felt to be important as a means of guarding against the possibility that the Russians might try to divide NATO by negotiating with individual members (clearly, therefore, there were lingering concerns about the possible use of Soviet-style divide and rule tactics of the kind discussed in Chapter 1). Solana's task would be to represent the institution and its member states as a whole.

Phase Three: institutionalised special relationship?

The second attempt at partnership

Conditions were ripe for an agreement that would entail the Russian government acquiescing in a first round of NATO eastward enlargement. In February 1997, Anatoly Chubais, the Presidential Chief-of-Staff, stated that, if a mutually satisfactory Russia–NATO document was signed before the approaching summit, this would 'open doors for future NATO enlargement'. He also pointed out that 'Russia has never said it was against any kind of enlargement',[76] which was true.

In early 1997, President Yeltsin also signalled willingness to compromise.[77] He did so at a March summit meeting with President Clinton, by accepting that a future Russia–NATO charter would be politically, rather than legally, binding: an acknowledgement that some saw as a significant victory for NATO.[78] Yeltsin asserted that, in return for concessions on NATO issues, he had secured a series of economic and commercial *quid pro quos* for Russia, principally in terms of greater Russian integration with, or prospective membership of, international economic institutions.[79]

Just before this summit, NATO members had also offered a 'Unilateral Statement'. This addressed a major Russian concern about the prospect of NATO conventional military infrastructure being moved closer to Russia's borders following enlargement. The statement declared that 'In the current and foreseeable security environment, the Alliance will carry out its collective defense and other missions by ensuring the necessary interoperability, integration and capability for reinforcement rather than by additional permanent stationing of substantial combat forces.'[80] Although the Russian government would certainly have preferred 'concrete guarantees' rather than such unilateral statements, which could always be retracted in future,[81] clearly this was better than nothing. As such, it undoubtedly helped the process of negotiating a new agreement.

The actual negotiations, which had begun in January 1997, were formally conducted at two levels: between Solana and Primakov and between their respective deputies. Solana and Primakov held six rounds of talks between January and May whilst, in between these, the deputies kept things moving with a further five rounds of negotiation. Insiders reported that the talks were sometimes fraught and difficult[82] and eventual agreement in mid May evidently came as a surprise to some commentators. It could partly be attributed to the good working relationship which Solana had managed to establish with Primakov,[83] an impression confirmed by the pictures of back-slapping *bonhomie* that accompanied press coverage of the announcement that agreement had been reached. Success was also attributed to the extent to which NATO members had deliberately maintained a united front behind Solana and resisted the temptation to cut bilateral deals with the Russian government.[84] Most pertinently, however, success had been possible because neither side made a serious attempt to tie the other down to a specific interpretation of what the new deal actually meant. This was necessary in order to reach agreement within a tight deadline: before the NATO summit scheduled for the summer of 1997.

A special meeting of NATO members plus President Yeltsin was arranged in Paris for the end of May, in order to sign the ponderously titled 'Founding Act on Mutual Relations, Cooperation and Security between NATO and the Russian Federation'.

At the rhetorical level at least, the Founding Act gave the Russians a great deal. NATO signed up to multiple pledges that the Russian side had been arguing for. These included revising its core Strategic Concept, continuing to 'expand its political functions', and taking on 'new missions of peacekeeping and crisis management in support of the United Nations and the Organization for Security and Cooperation in Europe'.

More specifically, NATO offered an additional element to its December 1996 'three nos' pledge. Part Four of the Founding Act, on 'Political-Military Matters', stated that 'NATO has decided that it has no intention, no plan, and no reason to establish nuclear weapon storage sites on the territory of [new] members'. This was given comparatively little coverage at the time but it was, nevertheless, significant. By disavowing any intention of constructing nuclear weapons infrastructure on new members' soil, NATO was, to all intents and purposes, ruling out the possibility of moving nuclear weapons there, even in the event of heightened tension or crisis. The unilateral statement on conventional forces was also reaffirmed. The text of the Founding Act did, however, specifically rule out a ban on extending elements of NATO's collective military infrastructure, such as fuel pipelines, to new members.[85]

A new 'Mechanism for Consultation and Co-operation' was provided for in Part Two of the Founding Act. This was to be called the NATO–Russia Permanent Joint Council (PJC). It was, so it had been said, intended to be 'a council of 17'[86] and, hence, more inclusive than the existing 16+1 consultative arrangements which, by definition, presupposed that Russia was an institutional outsider. The PJC was to meet regularly at either ministerial or ambassadorial level and, to that end, Russia was to establish a Mission to NATO headed by an Ambassador. In this respect, its representation would almost be on a par with that of the NATO members themselves. The proviso was that the Russian representatives would not maintain a *permanent* presence at NATO Headquarters, as the member states did. Formally, therefore, the Russian representatives to NATO would be accredited to Russia's Brussels Embassy.

The underlying purpose of the PJC, it was grandly declared, was to 'build increasing levels of trust, unity of purpose and habits of consult-ation and co-operation between NATO and Russia'. In summary: the Founding Act did give Russia a special relationship with NATO, in the sense that its level of representation and rights of consultation were greater than those accorded to any other non-member state. Insti-tutionally speaking, its representatives would sit on the PJC on equal terms, at least formally, with their NATO counterparts.

There was a crucial caveat, however. It was stated that 'provisions of this Act do not provide NATO or Russia, in any way, with a right of veto over the actions of the other nor do they infringe upon or restrict the rights of NATO or Russia to independent decision-making and action'. In addition, Part Three detailed 'specific areas of mutual inter-est', which could be placed on the agenda at PJC meetings. The list was broad. Yet, the very fact that the scope of the PJC had been limited at all meant that, in future, NATO members could keep items off the agenda when they did not wish to have Russian representatives discussing especially sensitive or controversial issues.

The initial response to the signing of the Founding Act was mark-edly cool in some quarters in Russia, where the decision to sign up was interpreted as a defeat. An editorial in *Izvestia*, for example, argued that:

> Russia seems to have bidden farewell to a whole era and to any illusions that it could stop the military alliance from drawing closer to its borders. At times this touching scene [the Paris sum-mit] evoked the picture of a country parting with the role of a great power and consciously shifting to a new capacity.[87]

Writing in *Nezavisimaya Gazeta*, Andranik Migranyan, a member of the Presidential Council, argued in a similar vein:

> [T]he fate in store for Russia is to drain to the dregs the bitter cup of defeat and humiliation as the successor to the Soviet Union . . . a content analysis of the Russia–NATO act indicates that the

document establishes a new post-cold war arrangement of forces in the world, an arrangement in which Russia has been defeated and shown its place, and . . . Russia has in effect consented to this.[88]

Migranyan's main specific complaint, voiced in the same article, was that 'the NATO countries' fundamental victory is their refusal, on key questions, to make any commitments that might tie the organization's hands'.

In countering such accusations from domestic critics, the Yeltsin government argued that everything depended on the way in which the Founding Act worked out in practice. As the presidential press spokesperson put it, NATO and Russia were at 'the beginning of the struggle in interpreting the agreement'.[89] The lack of prior agreed interpretations might, this argument went, work to Russia's advantage if, in practice, it was able to establish a more assertive role in the relationship than some NATO members might have envisaged.

Concerns over this possibility helped to explain the doubts about the Founding Act that began to appear in the United States in the autumn of 1997. They were the exact opposite of those expressed by dissenters in Russia. Far from worrying that the Act had given the Russians too little, the American doubters were concerned that it had potentially given them too much.

Former Secretary of State Henry Kissinger was amongst the best-known exponents of this view. Kissinger's major concern was that, via its position as a full participant in the PJC, Russia would acquire a *de facto* veto over NATO decisions. He claimed that:

It will be argued that if the Permanent [Joint] Council deadlocks, the regular NATO Council remains free to perform its historic functions. That is true in theory, but it will never work in practice. Since, except for the Russian representatives, the membership is identical, each country will assess the grave step of meeting without a Russian presence in terms of its overall relationship with Moscow. Thus, in practice, NATO Council sessions and Permanent [Joint] Council sessions will tend to merge. The free and easy 'family atmosphere' of existing institutions will vanish.[90]

Such concerns were understandable in view of the talk from high-level members of the Clinton administration the previous autumn, about creating a 'superpartnership' with Russia. From the autumn of 1997, however, the mood of the Administration shifted perceptibly.

Whereas, in the period up to and including the Paris summit, the accent had been on the extent to which Russia–NATO relations might develop,[91] now the message was more restrictive. Testifying to the Senate Foreign Relations Committee (shortly after Kissinger), Thomas Pickering, the then Under Secretary of State for Political Affairs, and a former US Ambassador to Russia, avowed that in the Clinton administration's view:

> The PJC is a consultative mechanism, and ... consultation in diplomatic parlance means just that, talking together. It does not mean a situation in which you are obliged to negotiate. It does not mean you are in a situation where you are obliged to make a decision ... In cases where the Russians might suggest subject matter on which there is no NATO position, it is clearly provided that NATO is not required to undertake any such discussion and certainly can, if it wishes and chooses to make such a discussion, first agree among itself, its members, as to what its position is.[92]

The clarity that Pickering claimed here was, in fact, not as evident in the text of the Founding Act as he suggested. This, in itself, was a good demonstration of the studied ambiguity of key provisions in that document and the consequent scope for differing interpretations. Specifically, the Founding Act did not explicitly provide for NATO members to 'pre-cook' positions amongst themselves before taking them to the Russians, although such pre-arranged common positions were not explicitly prohibited either.

To be fair, there are also grounds for doubting whether the Russians were prepared to engage constructively in the spirit of the enterprise from the beginning. The very first meeting of the PJC in July 1997 was postponed (for one day). This occurred because the Russian representatives raised eleventh-hour objections to the chairing arrangements, despite the fact that these had been set out in the Founding Act, to which President Yeltsin had affixed his signature two months previously.[93] During the first six months of PJC meetings, the Russian representatives threatened to walk out several times. The Russian government also displayed a persistent reluctance to conclude an agreement on the opening of a NATO military liaison mission in Moscow, also provided for by the Founding Act.[94]

Nevertheless, there were indications that, by mid 1998, the PJC was beginning to show promise as a venue for useful and substantive discussions, at least on occasion. Colonel General Leonid Ivashov, Director of the Russian Defence Ministry's Chief Administration for

International Military Co-operation, warmly praised a Defence Ministers' meeting in June. He subsequently described this as having been 'highly appraised by both sides in terms of substance and transparency'.[95] Six months later, then Foreign Minister Igor Ivanov stated that Russia–NATO relations had 'come a long way, from distrust to mutual understanding and joint efforts to resolve the issues confronting them'. He paid tribute to the PJC in helping to bring this about.[96] Public assessments on the NATO side were also upbeat during 1997 and 1998.[97]

In retrospect, the decision by NATO members to go ahead with air operations against the Serbs over Kosovo in March 1999 – the subject of detailed discussion in the next chapter – dealt a blow to the PJC from which it never fully recovered. In his first official response to the bombing, President Yeltsin accused NATO leaders of violating the terms of the Founding Act and announced the suspension of Russian participation in the PJC.[98] The Russian government had some grounds for making this accusation. According to the Founding Act's provisions, both NATO members and Russia pledged to respect 'the primary responsibility of the UN Security Council for maintaining international peace and security', yet NATO had launched its bombing campaign without an explicit UN mandate. Further, the Founding Act pledged both parties to refrain 'from the threat or use of force against each other as well as against any other state, its sovereignty, territorial integrity or political independence in any manner inconsistent with the United Nations Charter'.[99]

The Permanent Joint Council failed completely to function as an early warning consultative mechanism in the critical weeks leading up to the NATO bombing action. NATO members had, allegedly, not wanted to 'complicate' their decision making over Kosovo by granting the Russians any kind of formalised input.[100] Thereafter, virtually every appraisal of the PJC was negative and gloomy about its future prospects. In reviewing the situation in July 1999, Peter Trenin-Straussov argued that the PJC had turned into a 'failure'. He noted that NATO members had been caucusing in advance of meetings and presenting their Russian interlocutors with pre-agreed positions. As a result, 'the Russians for their part, soon discovered that dealing with individual NATO member states outside the PJC was more effective and satisfying'. In consequence, therefore, 'the PJC . . . turned itself into a talking shop for rather stale dialogue'.[101] According to a report from the Parliamentary Assembly of the Western European Union in 2000, 'while in the PJC the Ambassadors and Ministers [had] merely exchanged information and views on developments [in Bosnia and

Kosovo], it was in the Contact Group that the real political issues were taken up'. NATO members were accused of being unwilling to routinely discuss 'main political issues' in depth within the PJC, as favoured by the Russians. The former allegedly preferred to stick to narrower technical matters.[102]

By mid 1999, there seemed little doubt amongst informed observers that the PJC had not, ultimately, succeeded in placing Russia–NATO relations on a significantly more co-operative footing. Trenin-Straussov called it a 'disabled child'.[103] A report prepared for the NATO Parliamentary Assembly, meanwhile, argued that NATO's 'dialogue with Russia remains thinly rooted'.[104] Russian analyst Dmitri Trenin captured the prevailing view when he wrote that 'the two years of the PJC's operation have not left particularly good memories, or a good working model for progressively closer cooper-ation'.[105] By the end of the 1990s, therefore, the second attempt at constructing a framework for a Russia–NATO 'partnership' seemed already to have failed.

4 The Kosovo crisis

Introduction

The Kosovo crisis, which reached a peak in the last year of the 1990s, undoubtedly represented, for many, the greatest challenge to Russia–NATO relations yet faced. In 2000, for example, Vladimir Baranovsky argued that 'the Kosovo phenomenon contributed more to the consolidation of Russia's anti-NATO stance than the whole vociferous campaign against the enlargement of NATO'. In the same year, western analyst Mark Smith described the crisis as 'a turning point in Russian perceptions of the West'.[1] The discussions in this chapter are focused on why disputes over the most appropriate way to deal with the Kosovo issue became so serious and what the underlying bones of contention were. Finally, a preliminary assessment is made of the extent to which the overall Russia–NATO relationship was damaged by the crisis. This, in turn, sets up the discussions in the first part of Chapter 5, which are focused on the aftermath of the NATO bombing campaign, from July 1999.

The diplomatic build-up

In March 1998, the UN Security Council passed Resolution 1160 on the deteriorating security situation in Kosovo. This imposed a comprehensive arms embargo on the Federal Republic of Yugoslavia (FRY), of which Kosovo was a province. It also threatened 'the consideration of additional measures', should the FRY authorities not prove willing to enter into a serious political dialogue over Kosovo's future.[2]

The Russian government was obviously prepared to go along with the terms of Resolution 1160. Had it not been, then it would have used its veto power on the Security Council in order to kill it. It did not do this, according to *Kommersant-Daily*, for two reasons. First, in order to send what it hoped would be a final warning to FRY President Slobodan Milosevic, and, second, because the government did not want Russia to be isolated within the Security Council.[3] None of this meant, however, that the Russians were happy to countenance the use of force, should Milosevic fail to comply. Indeed, differences on this crucial issue became the major source of division and discord between Russia and NATO over the subsequent handling of the Kosovo crisis.

In September 1998, the Security Council passed its second substantive resolution on the Kosovo issue. Resolution 1199 made a series of specific demands of the FRY government and the leaders of the Albanian population in Kosovo. For the first time, it called for 'international monitoring' on the ground in the province, in order to verify compliance with these demands. As with Resolution 1160, the text also threatened 'to consider further action and additional measures to maintain or restore peace and stability in the region'.[4]

The fact that its government supported this resolution provoked some dissent inside Russia, chiefly on the grounds that its terms might be used by NATO members as cover for military action against the FRY, without further recourse to the UN.[5] However, as Catherine Guicherd has pointed out, citing resolutions on Bosnia as an example, established UN practice had been that Security Council Resolutions providing for consideration of 'additional measures' 'have usually been interpreted as requiring further action by the Security Council to allow military action'. This understanding was given added clarity and weight, in the cases of Resolutions 1160 and 1199, by the fact that 'Russia and China both had accompanied their votes by legally valid declaratory statements spelling out that the resolutions should not be interpreted as authorising the use of force'.[6] It seems clear, therefore, that the Russian government expected NATO not to make any military moves without further specific UN authorisation – which would, of course, have given Russia the right to veto any proposals that its leaders did not like.

There is little evidence to suggest that NATO members were seeking to deliberately provoke the Russians at this time.[7] Rather, a two-track approach was apparent. On the one track, efforts were made to maintain a diplomatic alliance with Russia whilst, on the other, a NATO military threat to Milosevic was initiated, with 'Activation Orders' being agreed in October 1998 and maintained thereafter. On 26 January 1999, at a meeting in Moscow between Igor Ivanov and US Secretary of State Madeleine Albright, the two sides declared that they had 'decided to maintain close contacts on the matter of Kosovo in order to coordinate US and Russian support for a resolution of the crisis'.[8]

A significant deterioration in relations between Russia and NATO members did not become apparent until the Rambouillet conference got underway in February 1999.[9] Over the course of these negotiations, which broke up and then reconvened the following month in Paris, the souring of relations was, however, pronounced. Marc Weller, who was present at Rambouillet, has provided a succinct summary of the deterioration:

> Throughout the talks, significant rifts in the Contact Group were visible, relating to the political settlement, to the implementation force and to the threat or use of force as a tool of achieving a settlement. These divisions became more pronounced towards the conclusion of the conference, when a collapse of the talks appeared likely. In fact, one might say that towards the end, the talks were less about Kosovo and more about relations within the Contact Group.[10]

One important bone of contention between the Russian representatives and their western counterparts was over the Russian perception that, not only was NATO biased against the Serbs, but it was also now actively seeking to engineer a situation whereby the talks would fail, with the Serbs being blamed. NATO members would then, the Russians felt, have their pretext to begin bombing.[11]

Some western observers, for their part, suspected the Russians of being partisan too, in favour of the Serbs. Tim Judah, who covered the Rambouillet negotiations as a journalist, subsequently wrote that 'once the talks started, the Russians seemed to take a softer line on the Serbs, to the extent that many began to believe that they were acting as their attorneys rather than as a Great Power trying to solve a problem with other Great Powers'. Similarly, Marc Weller accused the chief Russian negotiator, Boris Mayorski, of acting 'almost in the way of a representative of a particular party to the talks'.[12]

After the launch of Operation Allied Force – the campaign of NATO airstrikes against the Serbs – on 24 March 1999, following the final breakdown of negotiations, the focus of official Russian anger was on the fact that NATO had not obtained, or even tried to obtain, a UN Security Council Resolution authorising its use of military force. Russia's permanent, veto-wielding seat on the council was one of its few, undisputed, contemporary claims to international influence. NATO thus appeared to be wilfully ignoring – indeed subverting

– Russia's great power status and, to add insult to injury, wilfully interfering in a traditional area of Russian influence.

Yet, the Russian government had scarcely helped its own cause by making clear from an early stage that it would not entertain *any* possibility of approving NATO military strikes on the FRY, even if the issue had been taken to the UN. For several months before the airstrikes were launched, Igor Ivanov had been quite explicit that, if NATO sought a UN mandate, Russia would 'undoubtedly exercise its veto'.[13] In a report published in 2000, the Independent International Commission on Kosovo concluded that Russia's 'rigid commitment to veto any enforcement action' had been 'the major factor forcing NATO into an unmandated action'.[14]

The NATO bombing: the extent of official Russian anger

When the Yeltsin government severed its structural links with NATO in the immediate aftermath of the launch of the bombing campaign, it was sometimes suggested that Russia had 'broken off links with the West'. In reality, the action was carefully calibrated and targeted and it did not amount to anything so drastic. Specifically, Russia withdrew its mission to NATO and suspended participation in the PJC.

Equally important, however, was what the Russian government did *not* do. It resisted calls from the Communist Party to terminate Russia's military presence in Bosnia, now as part of the ongoing NATO-led Stabilisation Force (SFOR).[15] On the wider diplomatic front, the Russian government maintained normal diplomatic relations with all NATO governments, including the United States, despite the latter being vilified in some quarters of the political and military establishment as the 'chief aggressor'. The Yeltsin government was clear from the start – and explicitly so – that its practical response to the NATO 'aggression' would be circumscribed. Thus, following the initial bombing raids, Ivanov stated that 'Russia does not intend to take any [military] countermeasures with respect to NATO'.[16]

There were three main reasons behind this policy of *limited* disruption of relations. First, the Yeltsin government felt that it could not afford – literally – to take any action that might jeopardise the financial and economic support which it received from western governments and via international institutions and agencies, such as the International Monetary Fund.[17] In spring 1999, the Russian economy had barely begun to recover from the effects of the previous summer's currency crisis. Second, there was the underlying fear of being isolated, or rather, in this case, of Russia isolating itself, from the European mainstream. President Yeltsin expressed this clearly, one month into the bombing. 'In spite of NATO's aggressive actions, we cannot break with the Western countries' he said, 'we cannot lead ourselves into isolation because we are in Europe and no one will kick us out of Europe.'[18] Finally, there was a sense of impotence, a feeling that there was nothing Russia could do to stop the bombing anyway. A 25 March editorial in *Izvestia* had summed up this feeling:

> There aren't any measures we can take. I certainly hope it won't occur to anyone to go to war in the Balkans. And we shouldn't recall our Ambassadors either. A break with America, a break with NATO would be far more costly for us than for the West. So we have to grin and bear it. The more vigorously we shake our fists, the stupider we're going to look.[19]

A diplomatic partnership emerges

In his first official response to the commencement of the bombing on 24 March, Yeltsin, whilst announcing the suspension of relations with NATO in the areas noted above, was careful to keep the door open in one particularly important way. He stated that 'the sooner negotiations are resumed, the greater the chance the international community will have of finding a political settlement. *Russia is prepared to continue working closely with the other members of the Contact Group for the sake of achieving this goal*' [emphasis added].[20] From the very beginning of Operation Allied Force, the best opportunity for Russia to avoid being isolated or marginalised, and demonstrate that it was not an irrelevant actor, lay in the diplomatic sphere. Thus, it was scarcely surprising that, from day one of NATO military operations, Russian leaders concentrated their energies on efforts to broker a diplomatic settlement.

First off the mark was the then prime minister, Yevgeny Primakov. Primakov put special effort into cultivating the French and, especially, the German governments. This was shrewd diplomacy. Primakov was almost certainly calculating that the chances of an acceptable settlement package being constructed would be enhanced if he could build a sympathetic coalition inside NATO, rather than dealing exclusively with the United States. Second, he may have felt that these two European NATO members would be more amenable than the US to according Russia a key role in the diplomatic manoeuvring. Finally, some observers also again detected a continuing element of the traditional Soviet approach of trying to drive a wedge between the United States and its West European allies.[21]

The second element of Primakov's approach soon began to show results. At the end of March, *Rossiiskaya Gazeta* quoted 'French diplomatic sources' as saying that 'the small door leading to peace in the Balkans has one key, it is in Russia's hands'.[22] One week later, the German Foreign Ministry stated that 'the German government believes that a solution to the conflict in Kosovo can be found only through close cooperation with Russia'.[23]

Following Primakov's efforts, President Yeltsin decided to intervene himself. He did so on 14 April by appointing former Prime Minister Viktor Chernomyrdin to be his 'special representative for the conflict in Yugoslavia'. In effect, this meant that Primakov, together with the Russian Foreign Ministry, was being sidelined. That the continuing diplomatic efforts were taking place in conjunction with a power struggle at home was confirmed when Primakov was sacked by Yeltsin the following month. Vladimir Baranovsky has argued that 'the coming parliamentary and presidential elections [were] always present in a very conspicuous way in nearly all the steps taken by the leading Russian politicians in connection with the Yugoslav developments'.[24] By the spring of 1999, Yeltsin had evidently decided that he did not want Primakov to succeed him. In addition, *Nezavisimaya Gazeta* opined that:

> It is clear that the President had to put all national efforts to resolve the Yugoslav crisis into the hands of a man who would be completely under Boris Yeltsin's control and who is so well known in the world that he can negotiate as an equal with Western and Yugoslav leaders. Viktor Chernomyrdin meets both of these requirements like no one else.[25]

Following Chernomyrdin's appointment, Russian diplomatic influence started to become tangible and apparent. This can be demonstrated by comparing NATO's initial terms for ending the bombing and the package – with Russian input – that was eventually accepted by President Milosevic in June 1999.

NATO's initial demands were contained in a statement released on 12 April. They were:

- a verifiable end to Serb military action and repression in Kosovo;
- the withdrawal from Kosovo of Serb military, police and paramilitary forces;

- the stationing in the province of an 'international military presence';
- the unconditional and safe return of refugees and displaced persons and 'unhindered access to them by humanitarian aid organisations';
- willingness to work, on the basis of the draft Rambouillet agreement, on a settlement of the political status of Kosovo.[26]

Two days after these five points were agreed, a 'German peace plan' was unveiled. Actually this description, although widely used in the media, was inaccurate. The proposals were not exclusively German. They had been agreed jointly by German and Russian diplomats.[27] The importance of Russian involvement was repeatedly stressed on the German side, although it suited the Russians to have the proposals presented formally by the FRG, in order to increase the chances of a positive reception within NATO.[28]

The proposals that were eventually adopted, within the framework of the Group of Eight (G8), incorporated NATO's five demands. However, there were also four significant additions, reflecting core elements of the Russo-German plan. These were:

- the 'international presences' to be deployed in Kosovo following a Serb withdrawal should be both 'civil and security' – NATO's 12 April statement had spoken only of 'an international military presence';
- these presences should be 'endorsed and adopted by the United Nations'. A UN role had not been identified by NATO on 12 April, but it was a key feature of the Russo-German proposals;
- the G8 agreed on the 'establishment of an interim administration for Kosovo to be decided by the Security Council of the United Nations'. This adopted another important element of the Russo-German proposals which had not been mentioned by NATO on 12 April;
- the 'demilitarisation of the UCK' (that is, the Kosovo Liberation Army) was identified as an integral part of an overall political settlement. Again, the 12 April NATO demands, which had been exclusively directed at the Serbs, had been silent on this although it had featured in the Russo-German proposals.[29]

Overall, as Dov Lynch has noted, the G8 package 'contained important elements of success for Russia'.[30]

There remained the task of forming a cohesive and public diplomatic alliance between Russia and the West, which would stand a decent chance of persuading Milosevic to accept the composite deal. In retrospect, it appears that the Yeltsin–Chernomyrdin team, in their desire to become an integral part of any solution, were pushing at an increasingly open door. In late April, NATO marked its 50th anniversary with a summit meeting in Washington. According to then US Deputy Secretary of State, Strobe Talbott:

> There was a real sense of tension building, not just over the Russian opposition to the NATO bombing campaign, but there was widespread feeling that that issue was going to spoil much else of what was going on between the US and Russia, between the West and Russia, between NATO and Russia. Remember that for the previous couple of years we have been developing a co-operative and quite promising relationship between NATO and Russia, and that was increasingly seen as in jeopardy.[31]

According to Talbott, President Yeltsin put through a telephone call to President Clinton towards the end of the summit. During this conversation, it was agreed that Chernomyrdin should negotiate directly with the US on forming a joint diplomatic package, which could then be presented to Milosevic. Talbott was appointed as the chief interlocutor on the American side.

Things now started to move quickly. Immediately after the NATO summit, Chernomyrdin and Talbott began a series of meetings designed to flesh out their common negotiating position. They were joined from early May by Finnish President Martti Ahtisaari, as the representative of the European Union. The final G8 package was agreed on 6 May 1999.

It was accepted on all sides that the Russian representative was not involved purely for form's sake or to make up the numbers. Chernomyrdin's presence in the newly formed diplomatic troika fulfilled two key functions. After a month's worth of bombing, it had become apparent, as Erik Yesson has put it, that 'NATO could not bring to bear sufficient leverage on Serbia by itself; other actors had to participate'.[32] The best-placed 'other actor' seemed to be Russia, with its historic interests in South East Europe and ties to the Serbs. Chernomyrdin deliberately played on this, telling his western interlocutors that 'if you want to persuade Milosevic you have to convince me first'.[33]

Following on from this, Chernomyrdin was able to develop a kind of 'good cop/bad cop' approach, together with Ahtisaari. As Strobe Talbott subsequently reflected:

Thus was born what we came to call the hammer and anvil scenario. The notion was that Chernomyrdin would be the hammer and would pound away on Milosevic, and President Ahtisaari would be the anvil against who the pounding would take place, so that Milosevic would know what he had to do in order to get the bombing stopped.[34]

It is noteworthy that Talbott himself did not travel to Belgrade during the diplomatic endgame in late May and early June. Rather, he left it to Chernomyrdin and Ahtisaari to execute their 'hammer and anvil' strategy. For this to be effective, as Ahtisaari said, it had to be clear to all concerned that the agreed negotiating position really was 'joint work by the United States, Russia, and EU'.[35]

According to Talbott, genuine unity amongst the negotiating team was especially important when dealing with Milosevic. The FRY leader was, allegedly:

> [A] master at what's sometimes called forum shopping, that means you go from one international setting to another and try to figure out which one is offering the best deal from Belgrade's standpoint and go with that one. [Thus] part of the logic of what became then the tri-lateral diplomacy among President Ahtisaari, Mr Chernomyrdin and ourselves was to basically close down the gaps that existed among the various parts of the international community.[36]

In the event, the NATO–EU–Russia negotiating strategy proved successful and Milosevic accepted the G8 demands in early June 1999.

In order for the troika to formulate and adhere to common positions, some degree of compromise on all sides would, fairly obviously, be necessary. Some analysts and commentators do not appear to have appreciated this. It is an inaccurate caricature to portray Russia as having been little more than the 'messenger boy' or 'post office', simply transmitting NATO's demands to President Milosevic.[37] As demonstrated earlier, the demands that were transmitted were genuinely multilateral.

One issue remained to be worked out. This was the nature and extent of a Russian military presence, working with NATO, in post-settlement Kosovo. Chernomyrdin had accepted that the international security presence should be NATO-led and this was incorporated into UN Security Council Resolution 1244, passed on 10 June 1999, which put into place the agreed settlement.[38] The details of Russian participation were effectively set aside for subsequent consideration, in order to prevent this issue from holding up the overall settlement.[39] What happened next demonstrated that, for all their diplomatic co-operation since the end of April, substantial underlying distrust still existed between Russia and NATO members.

On the day after Resolution 1244 was passed, some 200 troops detached themselves from the Russian contingent working with NATO on peacekeeping duties in SFOR in Bosnia. They undertook a pre-emptive march to the airport in Pristina, the provincial capital of Kosovo, arriving before the first NATO troops from the newly formed Kosovo Force (KFOR).

Various explanations for this so-called 'dash to Pristina' have been put forward. One of the theories advanced was that Serb forces, on their way out of Kosovo following the peace agreement, had arranged to give back to the Russians military equipment which the latter had covertly supplied during the conflict (in contravention of a UN arms embargo). A variation on this had the Serbs handing over to the Russians the wreckage of the highly sensitive US F-117 'stealth' fighter, which had been shot down during the NATO bombing campaign.[40]

In Russia, some explanations focused on the perceived need for President Yeltsin (assuming that the move was, indeed, ordered by him[41]) to pull off a dramatic international gesture to distract attention from political travails at home.[42] Others argued that it was designed to show that Russia remained an important player in South East European affairs.[43] It had a significant psychological impact on the Russian public, which had seemed quite humiliated after the NATO airstrikes and was deeply satisfied with this small act of 'revenge'. The dash to Pristina showed that Russia could 'do something' in a tangible way. Russian media coverage was very positive; tearful Serbs with flowers greeted Russian soldiers on armoured personnel carriers, just like when the Soviets had 'liberated' Central Europe from fascism in 1944–5.[44] In addition, for many Serbs who doubted the ability – or even desire – of NATO and KFOR to protect them from vengeful Albanians, the arrival of the Russians had important security implications.

Some argued that the 'dash' represented only the initial deployment of an intended substantial force. Its purpose was allegedly to occupy the northern part of Kosovo, the heartland of its Serbian population, and assist the Milosevic government in partitioning the province. According to this argument, the plan was thwarted because Hungary, Bulgaria and Romania refused to grant over-flight rights to allow the Russian military to airlift in supplies and reinforcements. In his memoir of the Kosovo crisis, General Wesley Clark, then serving as NATO's Supreme Allied Commander Europe, makes clear that he believed that partition was the Russian objective.[45]

If, however, the Russian objective really had been partition, then the plan was executed in a peculiarly ineffective way. As General Clark also notes in his memoirs, somewhat contradicting his own argument:

> [I]f the Russians really wanted to enter and establish a sector in the north of Kosovo, they could simply drive across the border [from Bosnia through Serbia], even if we blocked the airfield, and plant their flag. Reinforcements could be flown in to airfields in Serbia and driven in.[46]

Why, therefore, dispatch a symbolic force to a high-profile site in the provincial capital when a force could have been dispatched directly to northern Kosovo?

The answer would seem to be that the Russian bottom line was concerned with ensuring that Russia had some actual military presence, however small, in the heart of Kosovo from the start and, therefore, was not frozen out by NATO. Many in Russia evidently felt that, when the crunch came, they could not trust NATO and its members to ensure that Russia's role and rights were properly respected, unless Russia itself moved quickly to establish facts on the ground before NATO arrived. Thereafter, and like it or not, NATO members would be compelled to negotiate a mutually acceptable Russian role in KFOR. This, in essence, is what subsequently happened.[47]

By early July 1999, it was clear that Russia–NATO relations had survived the Kosovo crisis intact, if far from in rude health. At no time had there been a complete breakdown in relations. It could further be argued, ironically, that representatives from Russia, the US and Western Europe had, from late April to early June, worked more closely together than at any time since 1991, and on a major international crisis. Yet, the dash to Pristina had demonstrated the fragility and continuing lack of trust in Russia–NATO relations. This had been underscored by the failure, by 1999, of two attempts to institutionalise a Russia–NATO partnership: through PfP and the PJC. Overall, the fragile nature of the situation was possibly best summed up by *Vremya MN*. It opined that:

> During the Balkan war, Russia made the most important choice in our country's recent history. We didn't ally ourselves with NATO,

but, thank God, we didn't become its enemy either. Now, Russia and the West can become partners who may not have any reason to love each other, but have to work together if only because there's no getting away from each other.[48]

5 The new millennium

September 11, Iraq and the NATO–Russia Council

Introduction

The first years of the current millennium have brought singular challenges to relations between Russia and NATO. Two events have been of particular significance in this context. They are the terrorist strikes against the US on September 11 2001 and the Iraq crisis in 2002–3. The discussions in this chapter, therefore, will focus on relations between Russia and NATO during the early 2000s, with special attention being paid to these two pivotal events. Before embarking on this, however, it is necessary to first examine the course of relations from the immediate aftermath of the 1999 Kosovo crisis to the eve of September 11 2001.

Russia–NATO relations: from Kosovo to September 11

At the beginning of Chapter 4, it was noted that many analysts had argued that the Kosovo crisis represented the greatest challenge to Russia–NATO relations to date. A minority took a different view, however. Thus, for example, in reviewing the course of the crisis in 2000, Ivo Daalder and Michael O'Hanlon argued that its overall impact on the relationship was likely to be 'modest'.[1] The discussions in Chapter 4 can be seen as lending early weight to this contention, given their emphasis on the ultimately circumscribed nature of the official Russian anger with NATO and the fairly rapid emergence of a crucial diplomatic partnership, which brought together NATO's leading member (the US) and Russia and proved instrumental in brokering an end to the crisis. Following on from this, the first section here will briefly examine the course of relations from July 1999 to, in effect, 10 September 2001 in order to assess more closely the longer-term impact of the crisis on the Russia–NATO relationship.

This period was characterised by a deliberate policy of incrementally restoring links and co-operation with NATO on the part of the Russian government. The process was begun during the last months of the Yeltsin administration. The first move, noted in Chapter 4, came when representatives from Russia and NATO agreed on arrangements for a Russian contribution to KFOR, in the wake of the 'dash to Pristina'. Co-operation in this area necessitated re-establishing some kind of institutional channel of communication between Russia and NATO at the political level, to allow for discussion of KFOR-related issues.

On 23 July 1999, the NATO–Russia Permanent Joint Council (PJC) met for the first time since before the start of Operation Allied Force. The Russian side was at pains to make clear, however, that this meeting did not signal a return to business as usual. Rather, the Russian government emphasised that the PJC was being reactivated for the sole purpose of discussing issues 'in a clearly defined sphere: interaction within the framework of KFOR'.[2] A moderate upgrading was announced two months later, when the Russian government decided to send back its chief military representative to NATO. However, it reaffirmed that this signalled no change to its basic approach of restricting contacts to those considered necessary in order to maintain Russia's voice in KFOR-related matters.[3] By the autumn of 1999, therefore, Russia–NATO links had been restored at a baseline level, but they were deliberately limited and restricted by the Russian side. Oksana Antonenko has described relations at that time as merely having returned to 'their pre-Founding Act state'.[4]

No further progress proved possible during the remainder of the Yeltsin era. Not only were negative memories of NATO's 'aggression' still too fresh, but the incumbent regime was widely regarded as having entered the twilight zone. The President was casting around for a favoured successor and seeking to make his exit in the most dignified and least personally costly way possible. It was, therefore, widely assumed that no progress would be possible until after the forthcoming parliamentary and presidential elections.[5]

Even so, Russian leaders accepted that their state would have to learn (again) to live with NATO on the European stage. As then Foreign Minister Igor Ivanov expressed it in October 1999: 'like it or not, NATO is a reality in today's international arena, primarily in Europe but also in the world in general. That's why we concluded the Founding Act on Russia–NATO relations in 1997, although it wasn't easy.' Four months later, former Prime Minister Yevgeny Primakov expressed a similar view: 'we have to talk, as NATO is a real force and this should be taken into account'.[6] Once the elections were out of the way, therefore, and a new President installed, it seemed likely that, notwithstanding the bitterness left by the Kosovo crisis, Russia's political leaders would continue the process of gradually re-establishing links and ties with NATO.

President Yeltsin announced his resignation at the end of 1999, having, it was widely assumed, manoeuvred his preferred successor, Vladimir Putin, into pole position for the forthcoming presidential election. Putin wasted little time, early in 2000, in making clear his interest in not only continuing with the restoration of ties with NATO, but also in moving them forward in qualitative terms. In February, the then NATO Secretary-General, Lord Robertson, visited Moscow on the first high-level NATO official trip to Russia since Operation Allied Force. He met with Putin and Ivanov and the two sides agreed on a statement pledging to 'intensify their dialogue in the Permanent Joint Council ... on a wide range of security issues that will enable NATO and Russia to address the challenges that lie ahead and to make their mutual cooperation a cornerstone of European security'.[7] Therefore, it was agreed that consultations within the PJC would, from henceforth, take place on other issues – in addition to those relating to KFOR.

Robertson was careful to avoid giving the impression of triumphalism over this agreement. He restricted his public assessment to the understated comment that 'we've moved from permafrost into slightly softer ground'.[8] Nevertheless, there was little doubt that this was the most significant step forward since the end of the NATO Kosovo campaign. In Russia, *Segodnya* asserted that 'it's safe to say that the crisis in Russia–NATO relations has been overcome, or almost overcome'.[9] At the first meeting of the PJC following Robertson's visit, a wide-ranging agenda was duly discussed. Issues included Russia's National Security Concept, NATO's Strategic Concept and arms control issues, in addition to matters relating to KFOR.[10] The broadened scope was maintained thereafter.

It is important to bear in mind that the moves made between July 1999 and February 2000 resulted in the restoration of the status quo ante, namely the PJC. Yet, as noted in Chapter 3, this had failed to function effectively when confronted by its first real crisis (in Kosovo). No thought seems to have been given to developing new and potentially more effective consultative machinery. The February 2000 Putin–Robertson understanding was premised explicitly on reviving the PJC and not on reforming it or creating some new institutional arrangements. Although the immediate crisis in Russia–NATO relations was thus overcome, the underlying structural and cultural weaknesses of the PJC had not been addressed. It was arguable that they could not be, given the institutionalised 'NATO+1' premise, namely that Russia was still an effective outsider within this framework.

In March 2000, President Putin made headlines at home and abroad following a television interview, which he gave to the UK interviewer Sir David Frost. Most of the subsequent attention focused on his response to a question about possible Russian membership in NATO. 'Why not?' was Putin's reply. This recalled the approach taken in the letter that President Yeltsin had addressed to NATO members in December 1991, at the start of Russia's existence as a post-Soviet state. Putin was, no doubt, intentionally emulating his predecessor in seeking to send a strong political signal to the NATO members at the start of his own period in power.

The signalling purpose of Putin's remarks was widely acknowledged, both inside Russia and amongst NATO governments.[11] This latter may have demonstrated a certain degree of 'institutional learning' on the part of NATO and its member states. In 1991, it may be recalled that there was no official acknowledgement of the Yeltsin letter. This possibly caused a degree of resentment amongst Russian leaders and policy makers, and contributed to the depth of their opposition to the subsequent NATO enlargement process.

In March 2000, Lord Robertson, speaking on behalf of NATO, said that, although 'at present Russian membership of NATO is not on the agenda', nevertheless, NATO members recognised 'the need for partnership between the Alliance and Russia, and will work hard to build on our existing links'.[12] Thus, 'partnership' was officially back on the agenda. Yet, it is arguable that NATO and its members missed the underlying signal that Putin was really seeking to convey – that the 'existing links' between Russia and NATO were not sufficient and should be superseded by something more substantial. In his Frost interview, Putin had stated that 'we believe we can talk about more profound integration with NATO, but only if Russia is regarded as an equal partner'.[13] This suggested a desire for something better, from Russia's point of view, than the PJC. NATO, however, was not prepared to offer anything more.

A sense of disenchantment on the Russian side with the perceived lack of substantial NATO follow-up may help to explain why relations remained marked by a degree of testiness during 2000 and early 2001. Fortunately, there were no further major crises at this time. On the other hand, from a NATO point of view, it seemed that, for every 'good news' story coming out of Russia, less welcome news soon followed. In February 2001, for example, agreement on opening a NATO information office in Moscow was reached against a backdrop of press stories to the effect that Russia had begun to deploy theatre nuclear weapons in Kaliningrad, on the borders of Poland and Lithuania.[14] And, in July, Putin told a press conference that, whilst 'we don't consider NATO hostile . . . we don't see any reason for its existence'.[15] Russia–NATO relations thus remained essentially insecure and their future course uncertain in the first years of the new millennium.[16]

The impact of September 11

Writing less than two weeks after the terrorist strikes on New York and Washington DC on September 11 2001, Henry Plater-Zyberk and Anne Aldis posited the view that the impact of these events on Russia's relations with the United States and its NATO allies might ultimately prove to be rather limited.[17] The discussions in this section focus on the extent – once the initial shock had subsided – to which September 11 had a more significant long-term effect on Russia–NATO relations than this initial assessment suggested.

In the days and weeks immediately following the attacks, it seemed as if their impact would be felt more in confirming already existing Russian objectives, rather than in ushering in anything dramatically new. In late September, President Putin was quoted as calling on NATO to admit Russia to membership – an echo of his interview with Sir David Frost eighteen months previously[18] – and there was consequent speculation about the prospects for eventual Russian accession.[19] There were also reports of exasperation at NATO Headquarters with the seemingly deliberately tantalising, yet ultimately non-committal, nature of Putin's remarks. According to Luke Hill, NATO Secretary-General Robertson, who met the Russian President in early October, told Putin to either 'fill out an application' or else 'let's not waste time with this'. Putin's response was, reportedly, to think things over for a moment and then agree 'to move on to more practical matters'.[20] That he had, in fact, done so was confirmed in subsequent statements, which called for enhanced co-operation with NATO, rather than actual Russian membership.[21]

The main thrust of Putin's efforts at this time appears to have been to take advantage of western – especially US – interest in constructing the broadest possible international coalition for the impending 'war on terror'. In this context, it has been argued that the Russian President saw an opportunity to compensate for Russia's overall weakness as an actor in the international system, by forging a closer and more substantial relationship with the US and its principal allies. As some have seen it, Russian foreign policy under Putin, post-September 11, came to resemble that pursued in the early 1990s under Boris Yeltsin and Andrei Kozyrev in its pro-western focus.[22] Many observers and commentators certainly seemed to be sufficiently impressed to suggest that a new era of partnership between Russia and the West was dawning.[23]

All of this appeared to afford the Russian government increased leverage to prod NATO members to respond more dynamically than before to signals in favour of enhanced co-operation. Following his meeting with Robertson in early October, Putin was quoted as saying that 'we have got the impression that our signals in favour of closer co-operation have been heard'.[24] Positive mood music had also been detected at a PJC meeting at the end of September.[25] Thus far, however, there had been little more than words. As one report put it, although joint communiqués from the two sides 'brim[med] over with warm words and good intentions', there still seemed to be 'little substance behind them'.[26]

The third attempt at partnership

The prospects of this situation changing, however, seemed especially promising from November 2001. Amongst NATO member governments, there had been talk that Russian representatives might be given some co-decision-making rights in a new 'council of twenty' at NATO. British Prime Minister Tony Blair was often credited with this idea, perhaps because he was reckoned to have a particularly good working relationship with the Russian President.[27] In fact, on a visit to Moscow immediately after the proposal became public knowledge, Secretary-General Robertson attributed similar ideas to the US, FRG, Italy and Canada.[28]

Robertson's public remarks on his visit to Russia were most noteworthy for his candid admissions about the lack of enduring substance in Russia–NATO relations to date. In a speech to the Diplomatic Academy in Moscow, Robertson said that 'the current state of NATO–Russia relations is not sufficient to deal seriously with the new security challenges that confront us today and tomorrow'. He offered an unprecedented public critique of the failure of the 1997 Founding Act to provide an adequate basis for a meaningful Russia–NATO partnership:

> Our partnership has remained a nervous one. The foundation for
> our new relationship was laid in the Founding Act, but the process

cf building upon that foundation proved to be problematic. Co-operation seemed to go hand in hand with competition. Funda-mental differences in perception persisted, above all regarding the future of the European security architecture, and the respective roles NATO and Russia should play within this architecture. The 1999 Kosovo crisis exposed these fundamental differences in perception.[29]

In effect, Robertson used his November 2001 visit to formally pro-pose the council of twenty to the Russian government. He also gave it a provisional name, the Russia–North Atlantic Council (RNAC). This new body:

> [W]ould involve Russia having an equality with the NATO coun-tries in terms of the subject matter and [it] would be part of the same compromising trade-offs, give and take, that is involved in day-to-day NATO business. That is how we do business at 19 . . . we get compromises. We build consensus. So the idea would be that Russia would enter that. That would give Russia a right of equality but also a responsibility and an obligation that would come from being part of the consensus-building organization. That is why I say a new attitude is going to be required on both sides if this is going to work. But if it works, it obviously is a huge change, a sea change in the way in which we do business.[30]

From these remarks, it was clear that Robertson envisaged the RNAC serving, in part, to 'discipline' the Russians. Hopefully, this might prevent them from repeating what some westerners had regarded as being a dilettante approach to the terms of the Founding Act (by, for example, repeatedly holding up the opening of the NATO military liaison mission in Moscow).

Was the RNAC idea a product of the impact of September 11 and a US-led desire to cement Russia into its international anti-terrorist coalition? A case could be made that something like it might have been proposed anyway, as a result of the decision taken by NATO members in June 2001 to proceed with a second round of eastward enlargement. *Noviye Izvestia* subsequently commented that 'NATO makes conciliatory gestures toward Moscow every time it prepares to admit new members'.[31] In any event, NATO Foreign Ministers for-mally endorsed the RNAC proposal at a meeting in December 2001. They stated that the aim of establishing a new council would be to 'identify and pursue opportunities for joint action at 20', by creating

'new, effective mechanisms for consultation, cooperation, joint decision, and coordinated/joint action'.[32] By promising 'new, effective
mechanisms', NATO members implicitly acknowledged that the PJC
had, to date, been substantially ineffective.

As 2002 began, representatives from NATO and Russia set to
work, trying to turn the RNAC proposal into something practical.
Their negotiations initially seemed to be characterised by familiar
arguments and posturing on both sides. The talks got underway
against a sense that whatever short-term fillip had been given to
Russia's relations with the West in general, and the United States in
particular, by September 11 was in danger of being dissipated. In
January 2002, an editorial in *Izvestia* argued that 'everything [is] just
like it was before . . . Sept. 11 changed nothing. The Americans are
the same as they were before. Russia and its president need not
expect a special approach, leniency or solidarity on the part of the
sole superpower.'[33] *Vremya MN*, meanwhile, commented acidly that
'the latest illusory honeymoon in relations with the US lasted less
than five months'.[34]

On the RNAC idea, the NATO position reportedly hardened in
the early months of 2002, under pressure from sections of the Bush
administration in the US.[35] In February, a widely cited article in
the *Financial Times* claimed that NATO had reached agreement on
restricting the scope for Russian input. Reportedly, Russia would not
have any kind of blocking power over matters pertaining to 'the vital
interests of any one Nato country' or 'issues that involve military
decisions'. Given the nature of NATO, this seemed to leave very little
of substance that could, potentially, be included in the new council's
agenda. It was also reported that NATO had agreed on a 'retrieval'
mechanism, allowing member states to withdraw an issue from the
RNAC 'if consensus proves impossible'. This would effectively give
them a right of veto over what could be discussed, although, in
fairness, the Russians would enjoy the same right.[36]

A sense of *impasse* was apparent in the early months of 2002. In
March, the Russian government was reported to have 'submitted a
proposal [for the RNAC] which focused very heavily on substance',
whereas NATO members 'had agreed a position that focused on the
structure, modalities and principles'. As a result, ideas for the new
council were 'still at a relatively early stage of exploration'.[37] In an
interview published in *The Times* in mid March, Russian Foreign
Minister Igor Ivanov stated that negotiations 'were not going well', a
situation that he attributed to 'the refusal by some to overcome Cold
War stereotypes'.[38] On a visit to Prague, meanwhile, Lord Robertson

had to fend off suggestions that the negotiations were being endangered by a Russian tendency to 'ask for too much'.[39]

Yet, the December 2001 NATO Foreign Ministers' meeting had pledged that the creation of the new council would be ready to be formally announced at, or even before, their next gathering, which was scheduled for May 2002 in Reykjavik. This imposed a deadline that would have been highly politically and diplomatically embarrassing – for both sides – to have missed. In Reykjavik, therefore, the NATO ministers did announce the creation of what was now called the NATO–Russia Council (NRC) to replace the existing PJC. Robertson's original RNAC name had probably been dropped because NATO members wished to make clear that Russia was not gaining a seat on the North Atlantic Council itself (this being the senior decision-making forum for NATO members only).

The details announced in Reykjavik were rather sketchy.[40] According to contemporary press reports, however, the NRC would give Russia co-decision-making rights in nine issue areas, including significant ones such as military crisis management, counter-terrorism, non-proliferation of weapons of mass destruction and missile defence. This appeared to confound the pessimists who had speculated (apparently with good grounds in the spring) that nothing of substance would emerge from the Russia–NATO negotiations. Some interpreted this as reflecting success for the Russian side in pressing for a substantial new initiative.[41] The agreed plan also provoked enthusiastic initial media commentary. In London, *The Times* called the NRC 'the most far-reaching change in the North Atlantic alliance since Nato was founded in 1949'.[42] *The Guardian* was only slightly less enthusiastic in describing the new arrangement as 'one of the most fundamental shifts in European security since the collapse of communism'.[43]

Important provisos were, however, reportedly included in the new arrangement. One was the retrieval or 'safeguard' mechanism, allowing participants to withdraw an issue from discussion in the NRC, if the prospects for consensus being reached with the Russians were judged to be uncertain. This would reportedly allow 'any single NATO member to veto any continuation of the discussion with Russia' in meetings of the NRC.[44]

It was, in addition, unclear as to whether NATO members would also reserve the right to formulate common positions in advance of meetings with the Russians.[45] This was an important issue and a potential bone of contention. It had been one of the main complaints from the Russian side in the PJC since 1997. Attempting to reassure Russian leaders on this sensitive issue, Lord Robertson had previously suggested that such 'pre-cooking' would not occur under the new arrangements.[46] Yet, barely a month after the Reykjavik meeting, Ian Brzezinski, Deputy Assistant Secretary of Defense for European and NATO Affairs in the Bush administration, was telling a congressional committee that 'the North Atlantic Council will decide, by consensus, on the form and substance of our cooperation with Russia'.[47] This sounded suspiciously like the US *was* seeking to maintain at least the option to pre-cook positions, if it wanted to do so.

Overall, it appeared as if both NATO members and the Russians had deliberately avoided trying to tie the other side down to agreed understandings and interpretations on all issues in advance. They preferred, instead, to reach agreement on the general principles and framework for the new council and to leave detailed modalities and procedural issues to be tackled once it was actually up and running. As the discussions in Chapters 3 and 4 here have suggested, the precedent for this – with the 1997 Founding Act – was not promising. The problem was that there seemed to be little practical alternative to, once again, adopting this approach.

Two weeks after Reykjavik, leaders from the then nineteen NATO member states met in Rome with President Putin, to formally set the seal on the new council. Their agreed communiqué was upbeat and effusive. The nine areas for co-operative endeavour, which had been flagged up in Reykjavik, were confirmed. It was stated that the NRC would 'provide a mechanism for consultation, consensus-building, cooperation, joint decision, and joint action for the member states of NATO and Russia'.[48] NATO officials publicly stressed the importance of the consensus-building element, confirming that a significant part of the rationale of the NRC was to educate their Russian interlocutors in the ways of responsible multilateral decision making.[49]

If this seemed a little patronising, it also represented perhaps the best hope of NATO members taking the new council seriously. The Rome communiqué stated that 'the members of the NATO–Russia Council . . . will take joint decisions and will bear equal responsibility, individually and jointly, for their implementation'. Taken at face value, this seemed unequivocal, although the recent history of Russia–NATO relations urged caution. The Founding Act was also supposed to have provided the means 'for joint decisions and joint action . . . to the maximum extent possible'.[50] However, this had never really developed, as has been seen.

Optimists could point to two important differences compared to the situation in 1997. First, there was some evidence that both sides had learnt from the failure of the PJC. NATO leaders in 2001–2 explicitly stated their willingness, from the start of negotiations, to bring Russian representatives more substantially into their core consensus-building processes than ever before. The Russians, for their part, formally accepted the implied obligation that this placed upon them to participate constructively and positively in the often frustrating and laborious task of international consensus building.

There was also the prospect of the NRC being institutionalised to a greater degree than the PJC. Russia was to maintain a *permanent* mission at the NATO Headquarters, as opposed to just sending representatives to meetings, as had been the case with the PJC. The 2002 agreement also pledged that a 'Preparatory Committee' was to be established to undertake the necessary staff-work in advance of NRC meetings. This apparently innocuous administrative announcement belied a more profound potential change. The Preparatory Committee would include 'Russian representation at the appropriate level'. This would, if implemented in good faith, allow the Russians to be involved in the crucial agenda-setting and preparation stages of the consultative process. Crucially, it would make it more difficult, in practice, for NATO members to present them with pre-cooked 'alliance positions'.

Underlying all of this was a perception, in some quarters, that western – and especially US – policy towards Russia might be in the process of undergoing genuine and significant changes, as a result of the events of September 11 2001. According to this view, the West was now ready to go further than ever before in bringing Russia into one of its core institutional counsels. In Rome, Lord Robertson spoke of the:

> Expectations that this will not be just another glitzy protocol event, but a real breakthrough. Expectations that the new NATO–Russia Council will not just talk but will act, not just analyse but prescribe, not just deliberate but take decisive action . . . and if we need a reminder of why, then there is a simple answer. There is a common enemy out there. The man and woman in the street, be it Petrovka Street or 66th Street, knows it, feels it and they expect us to address it. September 11 2001 brought death to thousands of people in one act of terrible, criminal violence. But it also brought a message to the leaders of the democratic world. Find solutions and find them together.[51]

Elsewhere, opinion was more mixed. Some commentators continued to argue that Russia–NATO relations still lacked underlying co-operative substance and that the new NRC was unlikely to change this. In the UK, *The Guardian*, adopting a markedly cooler editorial tone than had its reporter at Reykjavik, wrote of a 'phoney piazza of platitudes' in Rome.[52] The response from sections of the Russian media was similarly negative and sceptical.[53]

In the final analysis, uncertainty remained about the future of Russia–NATO relations, as did a certain unease over the likely durability of any institutionalised arrangements between the two, especially if a major new crisis were to erupt. In the spring and early summer of 2002, no-one was really sure whether or how the new NRC would move beyond the limitations of the old PJC.[54] Russian analyst Alexander Goltz set out a potentially useful litmus test of future success when he argued that:

> The problem is that we can come to mutual understanding and mutual decisions even without this body [the NRC] ... what Russia needs is the opportunity to participate in a decision-making process when [there's] some problem, some controversial issues, something like war in Yugoslavia. [It's] not a problem to reach an agreement when you have the same points of view. The problem is to reach an agreement and to come to a consensus when you have different views on the same problems. That is the task.[55]

The NRC's first tests

By the time the NATO–Russia Council reached its first anniversary in May 2003, it had survived two potentially severe tests. The first was the NATO Prague summit in November 2002. A central item on the agenda at this gathering was the further enlargement of NATO's membership. It was agreed to proceed with a 'big bang' extension, embracing no less than seven Central and East European states, which would join in the spring of 2004. The invitees included the three Baltic States, who became the first former Soviet republics to sign up to NATO membership.

When NATO had held its previous 'enlargement summits' in Madrid in July 1997 and Washington in April 1999, the then Yeltsin government had signalled its displeasure by ensuring that no Russian representatives attended, despite initial NATO invitations to do so on both occasions. Russian leaders had also previously expressed particularly robust opposition to the specific prospect of the Baltic States joining NATO.[56]

In 2002, despite reports of continuing opposition to NATO enlargement from prominent Russian military figures,[57] the Putin government sent Foreign Minister Ivanov to Prague to participate in an NRC ministerial meeting, as part of the overall summit programme. In a speech delivered the following month, Lord Robertson claimed that in Prague, Ivanov had:

> [O]ffered a glowing assessment, both in public and in our closed-door meeting, of the progress that had been made in the NATO–Russia Council in the past six months. And then he hopped on Air Force One, and rode back to Russia with President Bush, who was warmly received by President Putin. A revolution indeed.[58]

Perhaps even more significantly, the NRC also continued in business during the Iraq crisis of 2002–3. The course of relations between Russia and the United States, in particular, during this period suggested that post-September 11 relations had attained an underlying solidity and even a basis of trust, which would have been hard to imagine in 1999. For example, the announcement in August 2002 of plans for enhanced long-term economic co-operation between the Putin government and the regime of Saddam Hussein was reportedly greeted with 'surprising calm' by the Bush administration. According to *Kommersant*, this demonstrated 'a high level of trust in relations between Russia and the US' and it was speculated that the Russian government might even have given the Americans advance notice of its plans.[59]

In November 2002, Russia voted in favour of UN Security Council Resolution 1441, which was carried unanimously. This resolution famously gave the Saddam regime a 'final opportunity' to comply with a series of previous UN demands, stretching back to 1991 and threatened 'serious consequences' should the Security Council judge that it had failed to do so. This text kept the door open for possible subsequent attempts to negotiate a follow-up resolution authorising the use of force. It was reported not only that the Russian government claimed credit for promoting a compromise between those seeking immediate war and those arguing in favour of fresh arms inspections in Iraq, but also that it viewed the outcome of negotiations as attesting to 'the mature and partnerlike nature of . . . relations' with the US.[60]

Senior Russian political leaders were careful, in late 2002 and early 2003, not to be seen to be closing off any options completely and, thus, definitively antagonising the United States. In February 2003, President Putin indicated publicly that Russia might ultimately support military action against the Saddam regime, if it did not improve the nature and extent of its compliance with Resolution 1441.[61] Foreign Minister Ivanov, meanwhile, declared that his government would use 'all available political and diplomatic means to avoid a situation in which it would be necessary to exercise our veto power' in the UN Security Council.[62] This stood in stark contrast to Ivanov's bullish stance during the corresponding phase of the Kosovo crisis in 1998–9. Then, as noted in Chapter 4, he had consistently and unswervingly threatened to use Russia's veto to kill any attempt to secure UN authorisation of military action against the Serbs.

Would the Putin government, in the event, have actually been prepared to veto military action over Iraq? The issue was not, of course, put to a vote at the UN. What is clear is that, whether by accident or design, the Russian government avoided taking most of the blame for the failure of American and British attempts to obtain a follow-up UN resolution, explicitly authorising the use of force. Condoleezza Rice, then the US National Security Adviser, allegedly encapsulated post-war US policy as being to 'punish France, ignore Germany and forgive Russia'. Whether this particular phrase was apocryphal or not, it was chiefly the Chirac government in France that was demonised as the main obstruction by the Bush administration and its supporters.

The official Russian stance during the actual conflict in Iraq in March and April 2003 was essentially one of passive neutrality. It has been argued that this was the approach which, being realistic, the US would have wished the Russians to take.[63] In its efforts to 'forgive Russia', the Bush administration made a point of demonstrating continued diplomatic friendship and co-operation in the immediate aftermath of the conflict, in stark contrast to its short-term attitude towards the French.[64]

At a press conference following a ministerial meeting of the NATO–Russia Council in May 2003, Lord Robertson argued that the council could take some of the credit for ensuring that a rupture in relations had been avoided:

> I think that the existence of the NATO–Russia Council has prevented differences over Iraq from becoming a crisis, like the NATO–Russia relationship suffered during Kosovo in 1999. It has brought about a new maturity. It has created a new equality and a new respect for each other, so that we are now capable of disagreeing without falling out, of having different opinions without walking out of the room . . . the NATO nations and Russia . . . have established a working relationship of such durability that it can survive and move on from even passionately held differences of opinion.[65]

A sense of perspective should be retained here. The NRC had *not* provided a forum within which NATO members and the Russian government had tried to resolve differences over Iraq. It could not have done so, for the simple reason that NATO members themselves were fundamentally divided, with France and the FRG in the vanguard of those opposed to military action.

Nevertheless, the NATO Secretary-General was justified in his upbeat assessment. The Russians were far more constructive and engaged in 2002 and 2003 than they had been in 1998 and 1999. Why was this? One possible answer was suggested by Alexander Vershbow, the US Ambassador to Russia, in January 2003. Vershbow argued that Russian co-operation in the NRC was being 'facilitated by their perception that NATO is evolving in its orientation to deal with the very same threats that Russia is worried about – terrorism, WMD proliferation, and that's making it easier for them to see NATO in a more positive light'.[66] Just as it could be argued that western attitudes to Russia had become more genuinely open and amenable to its participation in NATO's counsels after September 11, so it was being suggested here that the Russian government, for its part, was demonstrating a new flexibility and willingness to co-operate.

The two were closely related. The Putin government seemed satisfied that NATO's declared intention to make the NRC more practically focused and more genuinely inclusive of Russia was being followed through. In the autumn of 2002, Igor Ivanov was quoted as saying that activities in the NRC 'have shown that this is not simply yet another mechanism, but something that works constructively for everyone. We don't hold empty discussions, but talk about what can be most effective'.[67] Alexander Grushko, Deputy Director of the European Co-operation Department at the Russian Foreign Ministry, echoed his boss. In summarising the ongoing programmes that had been developing in the council by late 2002, Grushko concluded that 'in a word, the Twenty is really working'.[68] Defence Minister Sergei Ivanov, widely regarded as being particularly close to Putin, told the press after the May 2003 NRC ministerial meeting that 'as regard to my assessment of this year of work at 20, I can say that we have already reached the practical, tangible result and there is less and less theory and more and more practice'.[69]

Building on the nine issue areas originally outlined in May 2002, by the middle of the following year, practically focused discussions and programmes in the NRC had developed mainly in four of them:

- a joint threat assessment had been developed on potential terrorist threats to Russian and NATO forces in Bosnia and Kosovo;
- agreement had been reached on a 'generic concept' for possible future Russia–NATO peacekeeping operations;
- a joint threat assessment was underway regarding the proliferation of weapons of mass destruction;
- the possibility of the shared development of Theatre Missile Defence (TMD) systems between the US, European NATO members and Russia was being explored.[70]

In May 2003, Lord Robertson identified the TMD discussions as being 'perhaps the flagship program' of the NRC thus far. There are two related reasons why such a sense of priorities might have been encouraged by the NRC's proponents on both sides. First, as Vladimir Baranovsky has argued, 'joint air and missile defence is by definition possible only between non-enemies'.[71] Second, as Robertson himself argued, hitherto, missile defence issues had carried the potential to cause major rows between Russia and the US and, indeed, between the US and many of its NATO allies in Europe. There had been some suspicion that previous Russian proposals to develop TMD in collaboration with European states might have been aimed at seeking to cause divisions between the US and its European allies in NATO. By developing an inclusive framework for potential collaboration within the NRC, therefore, such concerns could be, in Robertson's word, 'defused'.[72] In view of this, it is not surprising that TMD collaboration has continued to be given a high priority within the NRC.[73]

During 2004 and 2005, senior figures on both sides continued to laud the evolution of practical and operationally focused collaboration within the framework of the NRC. In April 2004, for example, NATO Secretary-General Jaap de Hoop Scheffer asserted that 'the expansion of our military-to-military cooperation has been truly spectacular – from 7 joint exercises and events in 2002, to a planned 57 this year'.[74] Three months later, speaking in London, Sergei Ivanov gave a detailed exposition of NRC-based co-operation in a number of military-operational areas, including naval issues, joint peacekeeping operations and military aviation.[75]

Yet, despite the generally positive track record of the NRC to date, it would be unwise to suggest that the 'bumpy road'[76] that had hitherto characterised progress in the Russia–NATO relationship has necessarily been replaced by smooth and increasingly effortless forward movement. There have been important instances where consultation within the NRC seems not to have taken place. For example, the deployment of allied fighter aircraft to the Baltic States in spring 2004, shortly after their formal accession to NATO. This caused a discernible – if, ultimately, temporary – chill in relations.[77] Several months later, President Putin returned to the subject in a question-and-answer session with western journalists and academics. He suggested that much of the chilliness could be put down to the fact that the Russian government was not consulted, or even forewarned, about this deployment. It felt as if NATO was behaving 'as if it was in the context of 1985 when the Soviet Union was an enemy'.[78]

The task for the concluding chapter of this volume is, therefore, to endeavour to define and characterise the underlying nature and quality of the Russia–NATO relationship, as it has evolved and continues to evolve. This task will be attempted through an exploration of various forms of the concept most frequently used by both leaders and officials in Russia, at NATO and amongst NATO member states, and by outside analysts and commentators, to describe at least their aspirations for the relationship. This, as noted in Chapter 1, is the concept of 'partnership'.

6 Russia–NATO relations
What kind of 'partnership'?

Introduction

In spite of the various problems and false starts discussed in this volume so far, the idea that some kind of 'partnership' is developing between Russia and NATO has become increasingly pervasive. The main analytical task in this, the final chapter, is therefore to examine whether any real partnership does in fact exist and, if so, what form it has taken. Before embarking on this, however, it is worth spending a little time considering and, ultimately, rejecting the possibility, which is sometimes raised, that the Russian government has not in fact been interested in any kind of partnership with NATO at all. Rather, some have detected official Russian interest in attempting to balance and constrain the United States, through trying to loosen its bonds with its core NATO allies in Europe. Elements of continuity with the 1950s are sometimes perceived in this context. As was noted in Chapter 1, it was often supposed by western leaders during the earlier Cold War years that one of the Soviet Union's enduring key objectives was to try to drive wedges between the US and its NATO allies.

A divisive Russian aim?

Some analysts have certainly argued in favour of this approach, or have, at least, suggested that differentiating 'Europe' from the United States is both necessary and desirable as an objective from the Russian point of view. Vladislav Inozemtsev, for example, has called for 'a restored bi-polar world with two poles, both found in the West'. In his view, these two poles of international power and influence should differentiate between 'the American and European forms of western civilization', with Russia as an integral part of the latter.[1] Ted Hopf, meanwhile, has detected – albeit without offering much in the way of concrete evidence – an increasing sense that 'popular and elite conceptions [in Russia] of what Russia is and should become exclude the United States from that image. Instead, it is Europe that is increasingly thought to be Russia's future, not the United States'.[2]

On the other hand, Angela Stent and Lilia Shevtsova disagree fundamentally. They argue that Russian leaders are more likely to empathise and, hence, work effectively with their counterparts in the United States, rather than Europe. This is chiefly because, in their opinion, both Russian and American leaders tend to share more similar views regarding issues relating to the distribution of international power and the use of force than they do with leaders in many European countries.[3]

Still others have contended that, far from seeking to exploit transatlantic differences and potentially put itself in a position to be able to choose between the US and Europe, Russia – certainly under President Putin – has geared its foreign policy, fundamentally, towards making a 'studious effort *not* to choose' (emphasis added).[4] Indeed, a perceived aversion to setting clear priorities and making choices has led to criticism of the Putin government in some quarters for allegedly having no effective foreign policy at all.[5]

On the basis of the brief discussions thus far, it will already be clear that there is nothing approaching a consensus amongst informed observers about whether and if successive Russian leaders should seek or have sought to differentiate or divide the US and Europe. Thus, it may be tempting to take such divergences amongst the *cognoscenti* as being sufficient, in themselves, to demonstrate that there is no firm basis for suggesting that Russian leaders have pursued differentiation strategies. It would be foolish to dismiss the evidence that does exist quite so readily however.

Senior Russian leaders have, from time to time, resurrected the old idea of a Common European Home, the origins of which were discussed in Chapter 1, in an apparent attempt to raise the possibility of US influence in European security affairs being diminished, if not excluded altogether. Thus, in April 1997 for example, Viktor Chernomyrdin, the then Russian Prime Minister, publicly stated that 'Europe is our home, we are masters here and must settle things on our own . . . of course we shall deal with other countries, including the United States, but it is for us, Europeans, to decide how to live in our home.'[6] In the autumn of that year, President Yeltsin raised similar themes in public addresses.[7]

Perhaps more pertinently, some observers detected indications of Russian attempts to undermine NATO's cohesion during the course of the bombing campaign against Serbia in April 1999.[8] In Chapter 4, reference was made to the initial Russian diplomatic overtures, with then Prime Minister Yevgeny Primakov in the lead. These had been geared specifically towards France and the FRG, in order to obtain their basic support for a diplomatic effort to end the Kosovo crisis, at a time when the US was perceived to be the main intransigent.

Nor has the Putin era seen an end to the apparent interest amongst Russian leaders in flirting with the idea of fostering and exploiting divisions between the US and its European NATO allies. Bobo Lo has argued that:

> The Putin administration prefers not to adopt the lexicon of geopolitics and, indeed, denies any agenda to undermine Western solidarity. But much of the purpose behind the European Missile Defence initiative, and Moscow's encouragement of developments such as the EU Rapid Reaction Force (RRF) and the Common Foreign and Security Policy (CFSP), is to assist devolutionary tendencies in Western security.[9]

In relation to such apparent 'wedge-driving', Margot Light *et al.* have made an important but often overlooked point:

> Western analysts and policy makers sometimes react as if Russia's hopes to use [such 'wedges'] were unnatural rather than simply unwelcome. They interpret it as a return to the Soviet past, or at least a sign of the potential danger that Russia might represent to European security ... The important point, however, is that wedge-driving is a rational response to a perceived *hostile* alliance. The way to prevent it, therefore, is to alleviate the perception of hostility that makes it a rational response [emphasis added].[10]

There is some available evidence to reinforce this point. The year 1997, which saw Boris Yeltsin and Viktor Chernomyrdin publicly airing their Common European Home ideas, was the same year in which NATO members finally decided to go ahead with eastward enlargement, an issue of huge controversy in Russia. Two years later, the NATO bombing campaign against Serbia was reckoned, by some, to have generated even more anti-NATO outrage in Russia. Small wonder then, if one accepts the proposition advanced by Light and her colleagues, that a wedge-driving strategy was possibly being pursued by Russian leaders and diplomats for a time in April 1999.

Yet, at no stage to date has wedge-driving been pursued by Russian leaders with a determination, drive and consistency that suggest it to be a core component of their policy towards NATO and its members. Rather, as Vladimir Baranovsky has suggested, it has remained a 'sporadic' element.[11] With regard to the Kosovo case, it is striking that the Russian effort, which started out as an attempt at wedge-driving, soon focused instead on getting the US involved in diplomacy, rather than seeking to develop a separate 'European' initiative. The key watershed in this regard was a Yeltsin–Clinton telephone conversation at the NATO Washington summit in late April. Thereafter, it was agreed that a diplomatic troika of three *equal* partners – the US, Russia and the EU – would be formed to negotiate with President Slobodan Milosevic. What was especially impressive about this subsequent effort was the extent to which it proved to be watertight and resistant to whatever efforts Milosevic made to find and exploit gaps between the Russian and US positions.[12]

With regard to the Putin era and, specifically, the TMD issue, in 2000–1, various statements emanating from the Russian government had floated the possibility of some kind of 'European' TMD system. This could be seen as an attempt to exacerbate tensions between European NATO member states and their transatlantic ally, at a time when the Bush administration's plans for a US-based missile defence programme were arousing controversy and disquiet. As time progressed, however, the Russian government adopted a more co-operative approach. Following the inauguration of the NATO–Russia Council in May 2002, the Russians agreed to pursue future discussions on missile defence issues, and possible practical co-operation, with NATO collectively within this new multilateral forum. In Chapter 5, it was noted that the then NATO Secretary-General, Lord Robertson, had lauded TMD co-operation as being the NRC's flagship programme in its first year of operation. In October 2003, it was also singled out by Konstantin Totsky, Russia's Ambassador to NATO, as being indicative of the extent to which Russia and NATO 'have taken very wide steps towards each other in the military-technical field and in terms of trust'.[13]

Therefore, the available evidence suggests that, at the end of the day, Russian governments, under both Yeltsin and Putin, have not, in fact, been interested in pursuing a *systematic* wedge-driving strategy. Rather, the objective in both cases appears more to have been to secure an institutionalised co-operative status – and hence influence – for Russia *vis-à-vis* the West. In pursuit of this objective, the Russians have proved themselves willing to work effectively with NATO in pursuit of identified shared goals, even in controversial and sensitive issue areas.

Can a similar conclusion be drawn (albeit, perhaps still tentatively, at the time of writing) with regard to the US-led war in Iraq in 2002–3? There were certainly some Russian analysts and officials who openly hoped to see that crisis bring about a situation that would, as one put it, 'transform the boiling discontent [with US policy] into a certain historical and geopolitical conception of Eurasian coexistence different from the one called Atlantic'.[14] On occasions, hints were given by President Putin implying that he might be sympathetic to such viewpoints and saw the crisis as an exploitable opportunity, to try to bring about a more 'balanced' world order. For example, on a visit to France in February 2003, the Russian President was quoted as saying that the informal diplomatic concordat that had been developing between Russia, France and the FRG represented 'the first contribution to the building of a multipolar world' and 'the first attempt since the time of World War II to find a solution to a serious international crisis outside the framework of blocs'.[15]

The discussions on the Iraq crisis in Chapter 5 suggest, however, that the Russian government was not interested in pursuing a course of action that might have produced a terminal rupture in its relations with the US. On the contrary, the Russians were perhaps more quietly co-operative – or at least not actively obstructive – than many at the time believed. Overall, it seemed evident that, in the build-up to the war in Iraq, the Putin government was content to see the FRG, and especially France, in the vanguard of opposition to the prospective use of force. In this way, it might hope to gain respect in Europe, and perhaps also see the transatlantic community weakened from within by divisions between the US and important West European states, but without provoking the United States into reviewing its own relationship with Russia.

The evidence suggests that this strategy worked reasonably effectively. During the spring and summer of 2003, the western press lauded Putin's 'deft diplomacy' and Russia's new 'influence' and 'leverage'.[16] Some commentators recognised that Putin was playing a tactical game. An insightful editorial in the *Independent* in the UK in October 2003 opined that:

> The French and Germans delude themselves that Russia is their dependable partner in a new anti-American bloc. It is no such thing. Mr Putin is a master of international affairs, the leader of a nation with an economy no larger than Belgium's but whose arsenal of ageing nuclear weapons – allied to its leader's personal political skills – allows it to punch way above the country's post-Soviet economic weight.[17]

Perhaps the best evidence of the Russian leader's tactical acumen lay in the extent to which the Iraq episode produced no significant lasting damage to US–Russia relations overall. Famously, as noted in Chapter 5, then National Security Advisor Condoleezza Rice was supposed to have described post-war US policy as being to 'punish France, ignore Germany and forgive Russia'. The seal was set on the 'forgiveness' in late September 2003, when Putin journeyed to Camp David for a summit meeting with his American counterpart. This contrasted with the then still frosty state of US–French and US–German relations. As such, it was almost certainly deliberately designed by the Americans to showcase the message that the Bush administration was, indeed, prepared to 'forgive' the Russians.

At the summit, Bush and Putin both went out of their way to put over the message that disagreements on Iraq had not, and would not, affect the substantive nature of their relationship or the co-operation and joint activities taking place between their two governments. Putin publicly affirmed the fundamental importance of the US–Russia relationship as he saw it: 'our talks today have once again confirmed that our relations are based on a clear vision and a clear understanding of special responsibility of Russia and the United States for ensuring international security and strengthening strategic stability.' He also seemed keen to emphasise that there had never been any real prospect of Russia actively seeking to detach key allies from the US, when he said that 'we have proven once again that our partnership is not subject to political deal making'.[18]

Russia and NATO: possible partnership types

The underlying argument developed here is that there is little in the way of solid evidence to suggest that Russian leaders have been pursuing a serious or consistent wedge-driving aim. Ultimately, this is because neither the Yeltsin nor the Putin administrations wanted to risk provoking a serious, or even terminal, break in their relations with the West. This is not to say that relations with NATO have necessarily always been co-operative or that they have developed a firm underlying basis of mutual trust in the period since 1991. That would depend on what kind of 'partnership', if any, has been developed. Before embarking on a more detailed discussion of the Russia–NATO partnership, therefore, it is useful and instructive to briefly consider the main possible partnership types.

The first partnership type to be considered can be labelled *pragmatic partnership*. This type, the basic outline of which will no doubt be familiar to realist scholars, sees relations as being motivated fundamentally by concerns about protecting national interests and national security. Whilst being willing to engage in mutually advantageous co-operation, therefore, each side remains primarily concerned about the relative power of the other *vis-à-vis* itself. So-called 'zero-sum' considerations will thus, in all probability, be a continuing part of the relationship. That is to say, policy makers on each side will be concerned that potential gains for their 'partner' may turn out to be losses for themselves.

As a consequence, a pragmatic partnership may well prove to be a tactical and ultimately temporary arrangement, rather than being more profoundly significant and enduring. Some, indeed, may doubt whether this kind of relationship really deserves the label 'partnership' at all. It is contended here that it does so because it presupposes the mutual management of relations in pursuit of the aim of preventing deterioration in the security situation to the extent that armed conflict becomes increasingly possible or likely. In this essential sense, the Cold War relationship between the United States and the Soviet Union, at least during the *détente* era in the 1960s and 1970s, could appropriately be described as having constituted a pragmatic partnership.

In a *strategic partnership*, as the name suggests, relations are motivated by broader agreement amongst the partners about the overall nature of international relations, the sources of potential and actual security threats and the most appropriate means of responding to these. Such a partnership is more likely to develop an underlying stability and ability to endure than the pragmatic kind. This is not to suggest that it will be *entirely* secure and immune to shifts in national interest and (mis-)perceptions about the 'other side'. At their base, strategic partnerships are still founded on concerns about each partner's relative national power, security and prestige in relation to other international actors.

Finally, if a *normative partnership* has developed, relations between the partners will be shaped in important ways by agreement on a common set of behavioural norms, values and standards. The focus may no longer be solely on dealing with external threats. As a result of considering themselves to be part of a 'community of shared values', the partners may also both claim and accept a right (and, indeed, a responsibility) for scrutinising the other's observance of the core norms and standards of behaviour. This might apply in terms of their own relations with others, even with regard to their 'internal affairs'.

An existing pragmatic partnership

The basic goal of Russian policy towards the West under President Putin has been, according to Dov Lynch, 'not to become a member of the Euro-Atlantic community or to merge Russia with it, but simply to align Russia with the most powerful group of states in international affairs'.[19] This constitutes a clear, basic definition of a pragmatic partnership. If Lynch's assessment is accurate, Putin has, in effect, adopted a 'bandwagoning' approach to alignment with the US and its NATO allies.[20] So too, it can be argued, did President Yeltsin before him.

The reasons why successive Russian leaders have chosen to adopt such an approach are not difficult to discern. First, as suggested by Putin at Camp David in September 2003, the prevailing view in the Russian government has been that long-term alignment with the western powers – and especially the United States – is an essential underpinning to Russia's claims to have 'special responsibility' for international security and stability. A fear of becoming isolated from areas of core concern and interest, especially in Europe, has also been an important influencing factor. As discussed earlier in this volume, concerns about the possible isolation of Russia were one of the key factors that helped to condition Russian attitudes towards the enlargement of NATO's membership and its decision to use military force over Kosovo during the 1990s.

The Russia–NATO relationship has also been infused with considerations about the power of the two sides, especially with regard to Russia's perceived relative weakness. Ultimately, loud Russian protests were not sufficient to prevent NATO members from deciding to enlarge its membership by bringing in former Warsaw Pact and former Soviet states. Nor did the vocal opposition and threats of veto at the UN stop NATO from deciding to proceed with the bombing of Serbia in 1999. For many analysts, the relative power imbalance has been an important factor in preventing the development of a more profound underlying partnership between Russia and NATO, especially between Russia and NATO's leading member, the United States. In short, they have argued that a pragmatic partnership, in the sense outlined above, is all that one may expect between essentially unequal partners. Thus, Mark Smith has written that:

> Although Washington is interested in a close partnership with Russia on many issues, it does not see any prospects for a grand partnership of two equal great powers, which would comprise the mainstay of the international system. The decline in Russia's

economic and military power makes it impossible to speak of a partnership of equals.[21]

In similar vein, former Soviet Ambassador Victor Israelyan has argued that a:

> [W]idening power gap helps to explain the failure of the Russian–US partnership to become the axis of international relations it was during the Soviet–US stand-off: Those relations were of a different quality – between equal adversaries. When it ceased to be a super-power, Russia lost its grounds for establishing equal, mutually beneficial relations with the only remaining superpower, the United States. This decline in influence has not been lost on US officials determining foreign policy priorities in the post-Cold War era.[22]

Notwithstanding this, and in view of what was discussed earlier in this chapter, it might be assumed that a pragmatic partnership is the minimum relationship that will develop 'naturally' between Russia and NATO, given strategic, geopolitical and economic realities. Yet, the existence of a situation of partnership relations of any kind should not automatically be assumed to be pre-ordained. In October 2003, Lord Robertson used the occasion of his final visit to Moscow as NATO Secretary-General to reflect on the four years of Russia–NATO relations as they had developed on his watch. He invited his audience to 'remember how difficult things were in 1999', when he had taken over at NATO a few months after Operation Allied Force. Robertson argued that 'although we [NATO and Russia] had had a formal relationship since 1997, it was a nervous partnership at best ... cooperation was too often grudging, reluctant and fragile'.[23] To the extent that a more robust and predictable partnership now exists, this is not merely due to some kind of natural evolution.[24] Rather, it is because the parties concerned have identified clear and important interests in it doing so and have made conscious efforts to condition their official attitudes and policies towards each other accordingly.

In his October 2003 Moscow valedictory, Robertson identified the events of September 11 2001 as being pivotal in helping to develop and solidify the 'nervous' and 'fragile' quasi-partnership that he felt had existed hitherto. Although it may, in itself, have been another product of Russia's relative weakness *vis-à-vis* the United States,[25] at the most basic level the official Russian response to September 11 provided what one Russian analyst has called a new 'minimum below which the level of partnership will not drop' in future.[26] Others, including senior Russian leaders, have been more expansive in their assessments. Interviewed in September 2002, Foreign Minister Igor Ivanov asserted that 'we [Russia and the US] have reached a more serious level in that partnership . . . the war on international terrorism . . . is what made Russia and the US allies again – for the first time since World War II'.[27] President Putin developed a similar theme at the September 2003 Camp David summit. In the fight against international terrorism, he said, 'we act not only as strategic partners, but as allies'.[28]

This apparent post-September 11 partnership is attractive to the Russian government for a number of reasons. First, it holds out the prospect of better satisfying the basic concerns of successive Russian leaders, as identified and discussed earlier in this volume. Namely, to possess and be accorded influence and status in efforts to deal with key international security challenges, especially with the US, and to avoid isolation or marginalisation, most especially from the mainstream of European security affairs.

Second, President Putin quickly discerned that the events of September 11 2001 offered an unprecedented opportunity to achieve long-standing policy objectives with regard to the ongoing problems in Chechnya, namely to get western governments to accept the insurgency as part of the broader international terrorist threat. It was hoped that this might lead to practical help for the Russian campaign to stamp out the separatist movement by, for example, governments in the US and Europe looking favourably on Russian requests for the extradition of Chechen exiles. It might also produce a reduction in the frequency and volume of western governments' accusations of human rights abuses on the part of Russian military forces in Chechnya.

Third, there can be little doubt that most Russian leaders genuinely hold the view that militant Islamic terrorism poses a significant threat to Russia's security.[29] This is not only because of the situation in Chechnya, but also because of Russia's relative geographical proximity to Afghanistan, Pakistan and the former Soviet states in Central Asia. In this respect, Putin was probably not being wholly disingenuous when he claimed, in September 2001, that:

> Unlike in the past, today Russia is working together with the West not because it wants to be liked or to get something in return for its position. We are not standing with outstretched hands and asking someone for something in return. I am pursuing this policy solely because I believe this is fully consistent with Russia's national interests, not in order to win someone's favor.[30]

Having thus articulated the view that the events of September 11 2001 and the ensuing Russian offers to aid the US morally and practically produced a new baseline for partnership, is it possible to state that the qualitative nature of that partnership has noticeably improved? In other words, is a recognisable *strategic* partnership now evolving?

An emerging strategic partnership?

The term 'strategic partnership' was first used in the specific context of Russia's relations with the United States. It made a public debut at a US–Russia summit in Washington in June 1992, when the first President George Bush and President Boris Yeltsin signed a 'Charter for American-Russian Partnership and Friendship'.[31] The administration of the second President Bush revived the term and started to describe US–Russia relations as a strategic partnership after September 11 2001. Senior members of the Yeltsin and Putin governments have also used the term to describe Russian relations, not only with the US, but also with other designated states, principally China. Interestingly, however, the term has not as yet been generally applied specifically to the Russia–NATO relationship. This is in spite of some evidence – discussed below – that this relationship might be exhibiting key elements of a strategic partnership.

The term 'strategic partnership' has seemed to some to be used too vaguely and in such poorly defined ways as to prevent it denoting anything useful or meaningful in the real world. Viktor Kremeniuk, for example, has charged that the notion of strategic partnership has basically been an invention of western think-tanks, aided and abetted by their Russian counterparts. For him, the concept is simply 'filled with hot air'.[32] To the extent that it has had any practical utility, it basically:

> [S]creened Yeltsin and his cronies' desire to get access to the rich Western resources. In exchange Russia was prepared to play a role of a Western 'partner' in limiting strategic armaments and non-proliferating weapons of mass destruction while the Soviet military giant was falling apart.[33]

Tellingly, it may be recalled that President Putin spoke at his September 2003 summit with President Bush of the US and Russia acting 'not only as strategic partners, but as allies' in combating international terrorism. This choice of words suggested that, for the Russian President, a strategic partnership was seen as being a step down from a traditional alliance between states. His clear inference was that a more encompassing alliance with the US would be preferable, from the Russian point of view. Realistically, however, Putin seemed to accept that this was unlikely to be achieved, at least in an institutionalised or *de jure* sense,[34] even in the post-September 11 environment. Since 1991, and mainly for the power-related reasons noted above, no US administration has yet been willing to accord Russia the status of being a full-blown ally.[35]

None of this necessarily means that their contemporary strategic partnerships[36] are devoid of all real substance for Russia's leaders. Andrew Kuchins has argued that, on the contrary:

> Russia today enjoys no alliance relationship with any state remotely resembling a great power. Not since the short-lived Sino-Soviet alliance of the 1950s has Moscow embraced another great power in an alliance relationship, and since the dissolution of the Warsaw Pact, Russia has been bereft of alliance partners except those that are failed or failing states. For a country like the United States, in the enviable position of strong alliance relations with powerful states, it is easy to be dismissive of the more vague notion of 'strategic partnerships'. But for Russia, these are very significant relationships.[37]

Notwithstanding this, however, Anatol Lieven has argued that 'a tremendous surface warming' in US–Russia relations in the immediate aftermath of September 11 should not, in itself, be taken as an indication that an underlying or longer-term *rapprochement* is underway. In Lieven's view, Putin's offer of support to the US in 2001 was motivated by a, quite possibly temporary, convergence of Russian and American national interests on very specific issues, such as the removal of the Taliban regime in Afghanistan.[38] The fact that there was an obvious – albeit not terminal – divergence in the American and Russian positions on important aspects of the international response to the next major strategic challenge (Iraq) would seem to bear out the views of those who argued that no substantial and lasting strategic partnership, still less alliance, was being developed.

There is a school of thought that has argued that relations between Russia and the US have continued to be only superficially close. There has evidently been good 'personal chemistry' and 'bonding' between Presidents Bush and Putin, but this has not percolated down or been sufficient to infuse subordinate government departments and staffs, still less their wider societies, with a sense of mutual trust and understanding. This view has evidently not been confined solely to the ranks of journalistic commentators and academic analysts.[39] In July 2004, President Putin alluded to it in an address to Russian diplomatic personnel:

> Relations with the United States . . . call for constant attention. We have objective pre-requisites for a long-term partnership here based on mutual interests, constructive dialogue and predictability . . . Good trustful contacts at the level of leaders of the two states contribute to close interaction, but this is not enough for a sustained and bona fide strategic partnership. The widest possible sections of American society, including certainly business, should be interested in constructive and good relations with Russia.[40]

Shortly before this, Alexander Vershbow, the US Ambassador to Russia, had argued publicly that the relationship between the US and Russia:

> Is still more broad than deep, and it is still vulnerable to unexpected shocks and crises that could knock us off course. We need both to institutionalise cooperation to a greater degree among our two bureaucracies, where Cold War thinking and suspicion may still linger, and to broaden the agenda so that both countries have a more concrete stake in our partnership.[41]

The NATO factor

Ironically, in view of the frequency with which Russia's relations with NATO have been depicted in some quarters as constituting one of the principal problem issues in the post-Cold War European security arena, it is in this area that indications that a genuine strategic partnership might at last be starting to emerge have, arguably, been most apparent. At its heart has been the NATO–Russia Council.

As argued in Chapter 5, the NRC has developed, since 2002, in ways that are proving to be highly satisfactory to all parties. During 2003 (the first full year of the NRC's operation), it became apparent that co-operation was developing in a growing number of important and practical issue areas. Of greatest significance were the indications that, underpinning this practical co-operation, a *rapprochement* on formerly divisive issues, coupled with shared assessments of the sources and nature of international security threats, was also being developed. The most significant areas of emerging Russia–NATO co-operation to date have been, as noted in Chapter 5, theatre missile defence (TMD), intelligence sharing with regard to potential terrorist threats, and joint political concepts for future Russia–NATO peacekeeping operations. Finally, and reflecting what NATO Secretary-General Robertson called 'the most remarkable progress of all' in view of divergences over Iraq, efforts are underway to produce a common assessment of threats emanating from the proliferation of Weapons of Mass Destruction (WMD).[42]

As noted also in Chapter 5, positive rhetoric has been in evidence on both sides. Thus, for example, in May 2003, Foreign Minister Ivanov declared that the Russia–NATO relationship was 'becoming one of the pillars of the international security system'.[43] The following month saw *Vremya Novostei* asserting that 'Russia and NATO have become all but allies'.[44] In October, Lord Robertson claimed that the most significant recent development in Russia–NATO relations was a new underlying solidity:

> In the past each and every international crisis threatened to undermine the entire relationship. Today, the partnership is judged on its own merits. And those merits are strong enough to ensure that the partnership survives, and indeed thrives, in this new and more volatile international environment.[45]

Coupled with this, and of potentially the greatest significance in the wider strategic and international context, there have been growing indications that the Russian government and armed forces were prepared to make available practical support and assistance to NATO military operations in Afghanistan and even Iraq.[46] The Russian government reportedly presented NATO with indications of how it was prepared to help support its operations in Afghanistan at the beginning of 2003. Russian assistance, in practice, focused on intelligence sharing with the US and granting transit rights for German military *matériel* to pass through Russia en route to Afghanistan. There was no lessening of co-operation after the International Security Assistance Force in Kabul became a 'formal' NATO operation in August 2003.[47] If anything, the indications from Russian leaders and senior officials were that *more* help was on offer, if NATO wished to avail itself of it.[48] One practical consequence of this was the offer made by the Russian government during 2004 to contribute to NATO's Operation Active Endeavour. This is a maritime patrol operation in the Mediterranean, which had been activated as part of a package of measures agreed by NATO in the immediate aftermath of the September 11 attacks in

2001.[49] By late 2004, practical preparations – in the form of a joint Russia–NATO naval exercise – were underway to prepare for a Russian contribution to this operation.[50]

Yet, the indefinite continuation of post-September 11 operational co-operation cannot be assumed. In October 2003, following demands from the Russian Defence Ministry that the US military presence in Central Asia be terminated once operations in Afghanistan were completed, President Putin journeyed to Kyrgyzstan to open a new Russian military base there. Much was made, in both the Russian and western media, of the fact that this was the first new Russian military installation in a foreign country since 1991, one that was only twenty miles from a major American base in the same country. Though this development was probably primarily intended to be symbolic, the symbolism was potent. It seemed deliberately designed to remind the US and its NATO allies not to take ongoing Russian co-operation and acquiescence in developments in the war on terror for granted.[51]

A future normative partnership?

The 'community of shared norms and values' that allegedly binds together states in Europe and North America, and finds its institutional expression through NATO, is often discussed, but rather less frequently defined. Before considering whether and to what extent Russia is or can become part of this community, therefore, it is useful to recall the working definitions outlined in Chapter 1. These will then inform the ensuing discussions in this chapter.

Briefly, a basic security community, as famously first defined by Karl Deutsch *et al.* in 1957, denotes a region or other area within which military conflict between states has effectively become impossible. This may also be – though not necessarily – a civic community, in the sense in which that concept has been defined by Michael Brenner. In his view, such a co-operative community is based fundamentally and explicitly on shared norms and values.

The norms and values most often described by Brenner and others as forming the essential foundations of the contemporary transatlantic security and civic communities are individual freedom, political democracy and the rule of law. These are written into the preamble of the NATO treaty of 1949. This speaks of 'the freedom, common heritage and civilisation of their [the signatory states] peoples, founded on the principles of democracy, individual liberty and the rule of law'.[52] They also feature in the core treaties of the European Union. The preamble to the 1992 Treaty on European Union, for example, speaks of EU member states 'confirming their attachment to the principles of liberty, democracy and respect for human rights and fundamental freedoms and of the rule of law'.[53]

The contemporary transatlantic community

Are the transatlantic security and civic communities still in being today and, if so, how healthy are they? This question has become increasingly pertinent. The 2002–3 Iraq crisis, in particular, opened the gates to a flood of speculation throughout Europe and the United States. Many saw the disagreements between the US and leading European NATO members (and the equally deep differences amongst governments in Europe itself) as either presaging or demonstrating a terminal rupture within the overall community.

Although dramatised by the 2002–3 crisis, the debates certainly did not begin with it. On the European side, there was already a sense amongst some EU member governments and EU officials that, as the European Union developed, it was evolving a normative culture and set of values of its own. Whilst these values might still complement those of the US, the argument was increasingly being made that they were, nevertheless, becoming increasingly distinct (see below).

Partly, this feeling grew from a sense of increasing self-confidence, or, at least, a sense that a larger EU, with growing responsibilities in the foreign and defence policy arenas, ought to be a more self-assured and confident international actor in its own right. A well-known early indication of self-confidence, albeit one that was to prove hubristic and, hence, ultimately ignominious, came in 1991. The onset of the disintegration of Socialist Yugoslavia presented to some West European governments an opportunity for Europeans to prove that they could successfully sort out a security problem in their own backyard, without recourse to the United States. This attitude found reflection in the (in)famous statement by Luxembourg's then Foreign Minister, Jacques Poos, as he set off on an early mediation mission. 'This is the hour of Europe,' he declared, 'not the hour of the Americans.'[54] Then European Commission President, Jacques Delors, expressed similar sentiments shortly thereafter: 'we do not interfere in American affairs [and] we trust that America will not interfere in European affairs'.[55]

Much of the rest of the 1990s proved chastening for the EU and its members in the foreign and security policy spheres. Its mediators were unable to stop the onset of civil war in Bosnia or to bring it to an end. That conflict was only ended when the US led a significant NATO military intervention in 1995. For some, the 1998–9 Kosovo crisis was an even greater humiliation, given the extent of US military dominance in Operation Allied Force (where it provided 75 per cent of the air-craft). Arguably, the fall-out from this latter crisis helped to concentrate the minds of leading EU members on the perceived need to finally become more genuinely autonomous *vis-à-vis* the US in the military arena. Thus, the proposal for a European Security and Defence Policy, which had been born at an Anglo-French summit in December 1998, was endorsed at a full EU meeting in June 1999.[56]

More pertinent to the discussions here, there were also hints from senior EU officials of a sense that core values and attitudes to the rest of the world were increasingly diverging between the US and certain EU member states. In March 2003, on the eve of the war in Iraq, European Commission President Romano Prodi told a French audience that the war 'could have lasting repercussions for European integration . . . because it calls into question the values we Europeans hold dear, such as our concern for peace, the rule of law and multilateralism'. Prodi also appeared to support the French government in its disagreement with the US approach to Iraq. He suggested that the former could claim to be upholding distinctly European values: 'by supporting the United Nations and the multilateral approach, by running the risk of saying what they think loud and clear, the French authorities are implicitly defending a certain idea of Europe, the idea on which European integration was founded'. Finally, the Commission President criticised what he called 'European schizophrenia . . . we Europeans cannot go on indefinitely expecting the Union to bring us prosperity and relying on the United States for our security.'[57]

Three months later, Prodi told an audience in Washington that, since the events of September 11 2001:

> We have witnessed a diverging perception of reality on the two sides of the Atlantic. Since the Twin Towers, America has been living in a post 9/11 world. And this led to your new pro-active approach to potential threats throughout the world. Meanwhile, the European Union is absorbed with the new situation stemming from the collapse of the Berlin wall – and the opportunities and challenges it brought in our immediate neighbourhood.[58]

Comparable perceptions were also provoking increasing debate in the US. Perhaps the best known of these have been the ideas put forward by the analyst and commentator Robert Kagan. He has summed up his core argument in media-friendly soundbite form: 'on major strategic and international questions today, Americans are from Mars and Europeans are from Venus: They agree on little and understand one another less and less.'[59] According to Kagan, this growing (and probably permanent) divergence is based on two factors. The first is the increasing 'power gap' between the United States and European states (and even between the US and EU collectively, in non-commercial and economic areas). In short, Kagan believes that the US has the capacity and, consequently, the appetite to respond robustly to perceived security threats. Europeans, on the other hand, do not. Second, and perhaps more fundamentally, EU members today 'are not ambitious for power, and certainly not for military power', in Kagan's view. He attributes this sense of power aversion to the searing experiences of the two world wars. These have produced a distinctive 'European strategic culture', which places 'emphasis on negotiation, diplomacy, and commercial ties, on international law over the use of force, on seduction over coercion, on multilateralism over unilateralism'.[60] Very few, if any, serious observers have predicted a complete breakdown in transatlantic relations. Both Romano Prodi and Robert Kagan, for example, have noted important areas of close and enduring co-operation.[61] Yet, the fact that the core *strategic* element of the overall relationship was the one that was being called into question is especially significant.

The transatlantic relationship, as a distinct and important phenomenon in international relations, had its origins in a basic strategic *rapprochement* between a group of European states and the US. It came about, first, during the Second World War and was expanded and consolidated during the period of the Cold War. This explains why NATO, a military security alliance, became the prime institutional embodiment of the relationship.[62] It was only once the basic strategic understanding (based on Article Five of the NATO treaty) was established, that a broader and deeper community of values began to develop amongst the NATO member states. These states thus progressively became 'memberstates'. That is to say, as noted in Chapter 1, their leaders and governments have inculcated and internalised a set of core norms and values, which begin to condition their attitudes and behaviour, both towards other members of their community and outsiders. Thus, if a significant degrading of the relationship's strategic component is underway (admittedly a very controversial and contentious idea), this is likely to lead to the ongoing undermining of the whole transatlantic community.

Russia and the contemporary transatlantic community

It may be recalled that one of the main underlying themes of the discussions on Russia–NATO relations during the 1990s was consistent Russian concern about, unease with, and frequently public opposition to the process of enlarging NATO's membership eastwards. By the early 2000s, the official opposition had become less vocal and noticeable. There was not the same degree and intensity of debate inside Russia about the 2002–4 round of enlargement as there had been about the one that took place in 1997–9. This was despite the fact that the 2002 enlargement decision opened the door to no less than seven new NATO members, including the three Baltic States, whilst the 1999 enlargement had embraced just three.

Officially, the diminishing objections to enlargement were attributed by NATO members and officials to the success of the enhancements to the Russia–NATO relationship (the transition from the PJC to the NRC), which had been set in place after September 11 2001. Not all observers were prepared to subscribe to this perspective, however. Some argued that Russian leaders were, in any event, less concerned about an enlarged NATO in the new millennium because they believed that the institution itself was becoming weaker and hence less important as transatlantic relationships frayed. This situation was, allegedly, exacerbated by the unilateralist foreign and security policies of the Bush administration. It was also argued that enlargement itself, by progressively diluting NATO's traditional military core, might actually be working to Russia's advantage.[63]

Yet, if the Putin government really believed that NATO was in serious decline, it seems odd that it would, since 2002, have devoted considerable time and effort to developing practical programmes of co-operation across a range of important issue areas, within the framework of the NRC. It is more likely that the post-Yeltsin era accommodation reflects other possible considerations. One is a genuine reconciliation with the view that NATO, whilst still dynamic, does not, in fact, represent any fundamental threat to either Russia's security interests or its international status. The other possibility – perhaps more likely – is that President Putin decided to abandon the counterproductive Yeltsin approach of drawing supposedly firm 'red lines' against NATO activities, before then having to make major adjustments or retreats when NATO members proceeded to cross them. This latter interpretation would fit in with the view that the key – indeed, perhaps, the only – defining characteristic of the Putin foreign policy has been its underlying pragmatism.[64]

Returning to the larger theme of this section, there is little to suggest that Russian leaders, to date, have been persuaded of the view that the transatlantic community, upon which NATO is fundamentally based, is in serious danger of ceasing to exist as a core feature of contemporary international relations. At the heart of the Russian debates covered in this volume has been the question of how Russia can most effectively and productively relate to and deal with this community.

Russia, especially under Vladimir Putin, has, nevertheless, striven to take advantage of the fact that transatlantic relations have clearly been in a state of flux since the late 1990s. At one end of the spectrum, Dmitri Glinski-Vassiliev, albeit without offering much in the way of hard evidence, has argued that, far from being open to inculcating 'western' norms and values itself, the Putin government has attempted instead to impose its own increasingly autocratic standards and practices on its NATO partners.[65] Perhaps more reasonably and realistically, it has been argued that a sense of flux and uncertainty within the transatlantic community has allowed the Putin government to claim a degree of leeway to 'pick and choose which of the core values and interests . . . Russia shares'.[66]

In the early 2000s, this approach was, according to some analysts, made somewhat easier because the Bush administration was less disposed at the time to promoting democratic norms and standards inside Russia than the Clinton administration had been. It was also, allegedly, more willing to downplay morally and legally questionable Russian activities in Chechnya, as well as President Putin's alleged drift to authoritarianism more generally.[67] From early 2004, however, a toughening of the Bush administration's line, at least in public, became apparent. US leaders, from the president down, were more willing to criticise alleged democratic shortcomings in Russia.[68] This, coupled with evidence of a *rapprochement* between Bush and key European leaders (especially in France and the FRG), may make it more difficult for Russian leaders to adopt an *à la carte* approach to western norms and values in future.

The essence of the approach adopted by successive Russian governments to the normative aspects of partnership has been 'to steer Russia towards association without moving so close as to become vulnerable to leverage'.[69] The clearest single piece of evidence in support of this contention has been the persistent reluctance of Russian leaders, in both the Yeltsin and Putin governments, to seriously seek membership of NATO (or the EU). In part, this has been due to a desire not to allow either institution to gain leverage over Russia's 'internal affairs' and, hence, compromise its sovereignty in the vital military or economic arenas.

In the case of NATO, the main challenge in this regard would be the integrated military command and planning structures, especially its conventional force-planning cycle. Participation in the latter requires a historically unprecedented degree of mutual transparency on the part of member states, with regard to their military plans and force dispositions. In theory, NATO members can choose to adopt a 'French model' of non-participation in this aspect of NATO activities. In practice, however, this would be a difficult choice to make for new members. It has been officially discouraged since the NATO enlargement process got underway in the second half of the 1990s.[70] Even the French themselves, under President Jacques Chirac, have partially rejoined NATO's military wing.

In addition, it is not clear why a state would wish to apply for NATO membership, serve a potentially protracted 'apprenticeship' through the PfP and associated programmes, and then fail to participate in *all* of NATO's core co-operative activities once it joined up. In practice, all ten new members that have joined NATO since 1999 have chosen to participate fully in its integrated military dimension.

Underlying these structural and institutional objections, some have detected a more profound reason why Russia is unlikely to become part of a true normative community with NATO. For this school of thought, normative partnership is impossible because the West constitutes Russia's 'significant other'. That is to say, the western states – and the value-based co-operative links between them – constitute the actor or pole against which Russia's own identity as a distinct actor in the international arena has largely been both formed and measured. There are disagreements amongst members of this school over such issues as how far back in history the process of Russian identity formation *vis-à-vis* the West can be traced. There is fundamental agreement, however, on the basic proposition that, although Russia needs the West in order to assert itself as an important international actor, *it can never become part of it* without significantly compromising its national identity, status and, perhaps, even its very existence as a functioning state.[71]

Not everybody agrees with this. Some have argued that Russia has, in fact, been moving slowly but continuously in a western direction, in terms of its identity politics, since the collapse of the Soviet Union in 1991.[72] There remains a dearth of concrete evidence in support of such arguments, however. More persuasive are the views of those who have argued that, on the contrary, there was an increasing sense of divergence between Russia and the West during the 1990s. Some have seen this occurring as a consequence of the rejection of Russian aspirations for NATO membership, assuming that these were serious in the first place. It has been argued that, by not 'validating' Russia's early efforts to adopt a western identity through NATO, the NATO members effectively (if, presumably, unintentionally) undermined these efforts.[73] It is, however, arguable that neither the Yeltsin nor Putin governments have really demonstrated serious and sustained interest in NATO membership beyond dropping occasional and opaque hints.

Ted Hopf has suggested that it was the NATO decision to use force over Kosovo in 1999 which 'drove Russia away from an identification with the West', though 'not necessarily in an anti-Western direction'. Hopf bases his case on the view that:

> Russians are loathe to submit to Western values that pose as universals, just as in Soviet times, the values trumpeted by the communist party were advanced as universal. Kosovo, in its way, has pushed Russians to understand the United States, and its dominant position in the world, as a kind of modern Soviet threat to their emergent post-modern identity. To the extent that the United States and its Western allies claim to be asserting universally held truths all over the globe, Russians perceive the kind of ideological oppression just recently, and painfully, experienced during Soviet times.[74]

Conclusion

Overall, the discussions in this volume point towards the final conclusion that the partnership that exists today between Russia and NATO is primarily of the pragmatic kind. That is, it is based mainly upon expedient and tactical calculations, and only really becomes operative when important interests are perceived on both sides to coincide.

Such a conclusion is relatively uncontroversial. Of greater interest and potential controversy are the debates over the prospective future course of the Russia–NATO relationship. Celeste Wallander and others have argued that the events of September 11 2001 have not necessarily created the conditions for a stronger or more profound strategic partnership to be created and sustained over the longer term. In Wallander's view, there is still, in the post-September 11 international arena, insufficient underlying agreement between Russia and the West over how to respond to 'primary threats'.[75]

Notwithstanding this, it has been suggested that there have been some recent indications that the conditions for a future sustainable strategic partnership between Russia and NATO may be in the process of germination. This has been due largely to the work being done in the NATO–Russia Council since 2002 on such key issues as WMD proliferation, theatre missile defence and the fight against international terrorism. Of course, it is by no means guaranteed that the degree and breadth of co-operation will be sustained. By the mid 2000s, nevertheless, there was arguably a better chance of a genuine strategic partnership between Russia and NATO emerging and enduring than there had been at any time since Russia re-emerged in the international arena in December 1991.

Of a possible normative partnership, there has been no real sign. It has generally been considered such a remote prospect that very few serious observers have hitherto cared to speculate about the possible shape of one, if it were ever to be developed.[76] It would, however, be unwise to *definitively* rule out the possibility of this situation ever changing in the future. It may be, for example, that Russia's identity becomes progressively more western oriented as a result of bottom-up, rather than top-down, developments. In one optimistic scenario, the ongoing inculcation by the Russian populace at large of democratic norms and values might, in turn, increasingly influence the attitudes, approaches and policies of its ruling elites.[77] Potentially also – if currently unlikely – there could be an unleashing of popular pressure leading to political change of the kind seen in Georgia in 2003 or Kyrgyzstan in 2005. It should also be kept in mind that fundamentals are not yet finally settled on either side. As noted above, the traditional transatlantic community has been in a state of flux, partly as a result of the end of the traditional Cold War order and, more recently, of the impact of September 11 and the Bush administration's response to this. On the other side, as Sergei Kortunov pointed out during 2003, Russia has still not really 'developed a feeling of its eternal national interests'. This, in his view, 'is why the problem of its national identity remains on the agenda'.[78]

Given the sense that a final settlement of key issues has not yet been reached, profound changes remain possible in the future. In the medium term, the more likely debates, however, will be over whether the current, and still tentative, indications of an emerging strategic partnership between Russia and NATO will be borne out over the remainder of the current decade.

Notes

1 The Soviet Union, Russia and the 'Common European Home'

1 The author here follows conventional definitions of the West to include the United States, Canada and the European members of the North Atlantic Treaty Organisation, a growing number of which are geographically situated in Central or South Eastern Europe. The other core 'western' institution is, of course, the European Union.

2 'Eastern Europe' was the essentially ideological label generally used to describe the non-Soviet members of the Warsaw Pact during the Cold War. Today, these states and their successors are usually referred to as 'Central European'. The term 'Eastern Europe' is now more often used to describe the Soviet successor states, widely regarded as being politically, economically and institutionally more distant from 'the West'. The position of states in the Balkans is ambiguous. Some, such as Slovenia and Croatia, are established in or moving towards 'Central Europe' in terms of their political, economic and institutional orientation. Others are more clearly 'East European' at present, though with indications that this position is not immutable. Examples here are Albania, Macedonia and the Union of Serbia and Montenegro.

3 M. Gorbachev, *Memoirs*, London, Doubleday, 1996, p. 428.

4 In 1994 it was agreed to rename the CSCE the Organization for Security and Co-operation in Europe (OSCE).

5 For a strong argument that divisiveness, in this sense, has been a consistent objective of Soviet (and Russian) foreign policy, see M. Smith, *Contemporary Russian Perceptions of Euro-Atlanticism*, Camberley, Conflict Studies Research Centre, 2002.

6 See 'The Choice for Europe', *The Economist*, 12 December 1953, pp. 791–2.

7 The Romanian government under Nicolae Ceauşescu, whilst a participant in the CSCE, subsequently declared that it did not consider itself bound by the human rights dimension.

8 *Pravda*, 24 November 1981. Translated in *The Current Digest of the Soviet Press* [hereafter *CDSP*], 1981, vol. XXXIII, no. 47, pp. 3–4.

9 N. Malcolm, 'The "Common European Home" and Soviet European Policy', *International Affairs*, 1989, vol. 65, no. 4, pp. 662–3.

10 *Pravda*, 4 October 1985. *CDSP*, 1985, vol. XXXVII, no. 40, pp. 7–10. For the 'realists' part see p. 10.

11 *Pravda*, 11 April 1987. *CDSP*, 1987, vol. XXXIX, no. 15, p. 11.

12 M. Gorbachev, *Perestroika: New Thinking for Our Country and the World*, London, Collins, 1987, p. 208.

13 Gorbachev, *Perestroika*, p. 208.

14 'Mikhail Gorbachev's Address to the Parliamentary Assembly of the Council of Europe', *Visit of Mikhail Gorbachev to France July 4–6 1989*, Moscow, Novosti, 1989, p. 64.

15 *Pravda*, 11 April 1987.

16 Gorbachev, *Memoirs*, pp. 428–9.

17 'Mikhail Gorbachev's Address to the Parliamentary Assembly of the Council of Europe', p. 63.

18 A. Collins, *The Security Dilemma and the End of the Cold War*, Edinburgh, Keele University Press, 1997, p. 149.

19 'Mikhail Gorbachev's Address to the Parliamentary Assembly of the Council of Europe', p. 75.

20 On the key role of the CSCE in Gorbachev's thinking see M. Saeter, 'New Thinking, Perestroika, and the Process of Europeanization', *Bulletin of Peace Proposals*, 1989, vol. 20, no. 1, pp. 47–57.

21 *Conference on Security and Co-operation in Europe – Final Act*, London, Her Majesty's Stationery Office, 1975. For a good contemporary account of Soviet motivations in proposing and negotiating for an all-Europe conference in the early 1970s see M. Povolny, 'The Soviet Union and the European Security Conference', *Orbis*, 1974, vol. XVIII, no. 1, pp. 201–30.

22 *Pravda*, 20 November 1990. *CDSP*, 1990, vol. XLII, no. 47, p. 2.

23 S. Lambert, 'Brussels invokes CSCE charter', *Independent*, 23 January 1991.

24 *Izvestia*, 21 June 1991. *CDSP*, 1991, vol. XLIII, no. 25, p. 21. See also S. Helm, 'Moscow keeps its crises to itself', *Independent*, 20 June 1991 and S. Helm, 'CSCE wins right to discuss Soviet crises', *Independent*, 21 June 1991.

25 D. Lynch, 'Russia and the Organization for Security and Cooperation in Europe', in M. Webber (ed.) *Russia and Europe: Conflict or Cooperation?*, Basingstoke, Macmillan, 2000, pp. 101–2.

26 For a brief but useful overview of the debates about Russian national identity in the early 1990s see G. Dijkink, *National Identity and Geopolitical Visions*, London, Routledge, 1996, ch. 8. For the views of a prominent Russian analyst see V. Baranovsky, 'Russia: a part of Europe or apart from Europe?', *International Affairs*, 2000, vol. 76, no. 3, pp. 443–58.

27 *Izvestia*, 10 July 1992. Translated in *The Current Digest of the Post-Soviet Press* [hereafter *CDPSP*], 1992, vol. XLIV, no. 28, p. 13. See also Lynch, 'Russia and the OSCE', p. 106.

28 Subsequently the CSCE, together with other international organisations, did get involved in dealing with this issue. See K. Aldred and M. A. Smith, 'Imperial ambition or humanitarian concern? Russia and its "Near Abroad"', *Journal of Humanitarian Assistance*, web text, http://www.jha.ac/articles/a025.htm.

29 See, *inter alia*, *Segodnya*, 6 April 1994. *CDPSP*, 1994, vol. XLVI, no. 14, p. 21; 'An interview with Russian Foreign Minister Andrei Kozyrev', *RFE/RL Research Report*, 1994, vol. 3, no. 28, pp. 40–1.
30 On this incident see S. Talbott, *The Russia Hand: A Memoir of Presidential Diplomacy*, New York, Random House, 2002, pp. 40–1.
31 R. Mauthner, 'Scare tactic by Russia stuns conference', *Financial Times*, 15 December 1992.
32 A. Zagorski, 'Russia and European institutions', in V. Baranovsky (ed.) *Russia and Europe: The Emerging Security Agenda*, Oxford, SIPRI/ Oxford University Press, 1997, p. 526. See also B. Clark, 'Russia and west split on Europe's security', *Financial Times*, 10 October 1994.
33 See K. Aldred and M. A. Smith, *Superpowers in the Post-Cold War Era*, Basingstoke, Macmillan, 1999, ch. 4.
34 See *Krasnaya Zvezda*, 14 July 1994. *CDPSP*, 1994, vol. XLVI, no. 28, pp. 22–3.
35 See A. Kozyrev, 'Russia and NATO: A partnership for a united and peaceful Europe', *NATO Review*, 1994, vol. 42, no. 4, web text, http://www.nato.int/docu/review/1994/9404–1.htm.
36 *Segodnya*, 25 February 1994. *CDPSP*, 1994, vol. XLVI, no. 8, p. 13. See also S. Crawshaw, 'Yeltsin calls for blanket security for all Europe', *Independent*, 12 May 1994.
37 *Rossiiskaya Gazeta*, 7 December 1994. *CDPSP*, 1994, vol. XLVI, no. 49, p. 8.
38 L. Buszynski, *Russian Foreign Policy after the Cold War*, Westport, Praeger, 1996, pp. 85–6. See also *Rossiiskaya Gazeta*, 8 December 1994. *CDPSP*, 1994, vol. XLVI, no. 49, pp. 12–13.
39 For general information and background on the Assistance Group, see *OSCE Assistance Group to Chechnya*, website reference, http://www.osce.org/chechnya/overview/.
40 Y. Ushakov, 'Europe: towards a new security model', *International Affairs* (Moscow), 1995, nos. 4/5, pp. 10–11.
41 On this see, *inter alia*, 'Tell it like it is', *The Economist*, 8 June 2002, p. 14.
42 Lynch, 'Russia and the OSCE', p. 115; Zagorski, 'Russia and European institutions', p. 526.
43 See W. Odom, 'Russia's several seats at the table', *International Affairs*, 1998, vol. 74, no. 4, pp. 813–16.
44 In December 1998, the AG withdrew from Chechnya because of the 'deteriorating internal security situation'. It is worth noting, however, that the Russian government made available temporary accommodation in Moscow so that the OSCE team did not have to leave Russia altogether. The AG returned to Chechnya in June 2001.
45 *Nezavisimaya Gazeta*, 3 November 1999. *CDPSP*, 1999, vol. 51, no. 44, p. 17.
46 *Noviye Izvestia*, 3 November 1999. *CDPSP*, 1999, vol. 51, no. 44, p. 18.
47 See, *inter alia*, *Kommersant*, 16 November 1999. *CDPSP*, 1999, vol. 51, no. 46, pp. 5–6; *Vremya MN*, 17 November 1999. *CDPSP*, 1999, vol. 51, no. 46, p. 6.
48 *OSCE Istanbul Summit Declaration 1999*, web text, http://www.osce.org/docs/english/1990–1999/summits/istadec199e.htm.
49 Lynch, 'Russia and the OSCE', p. 118.

50 For Ivanov's view see 'Russia: OSCE hopes US efforts may allow it to stay in Chechnya', *Johnson's Russia List (1–5–03)*, web text, http://www.cdi.org/russia/johnson/7005–12.cfm. For additional background and commentary on the non-renewal of the OSCE AG mandate see also 'Moscow ends OSCE mission in Chechnya', *Johnson's Russia List (1–1–03)*, web text, http://www.cdi.org/russia/johnson/7001–8.cfm; 'Russian pundits disagree on decision to end OSCE mission to Chechnya', *Johnson's Russia List (1–5–03)*, web text, http://www.cdi.org/russia/johnson/7005–11.cfm; 'Kremlin rules out international mediation in Chechen war', *Johnson's Russia List (7–18–03)*, web text, http://www.cdi.org/russia/johnson/7256–13.cfm.

51 Weight was lent to this view when, in July 2004, the members of the Commonwealth of Independent States, reportedly under Russian influence, issued a statement criticising the OSCE, both for alleged ineffectiveness and a tendency to try to interfere in the internal affairs of its member states. See *Vremya Novostei*, 9 July 2004. *CDPSP*, 2004, vol. 56, no. 27, pp. 18–19. For further official Russian criticisms, in late 2004, see *Kommersant*, 8 December 2004. *CDPSP*, 2004, vol. 56, no. 49, p. 11. See also D. Dombey, 'Russia and US reach OSCE deal', *Financial Times*, 11 April 2005.

52 *Moskovskiye Novosti*, 23–9 November 1999. *CDPSP*, 1999, vol. 51, no. 47, p. 6.

53 K. Deutsch *et al.*, *Political Community and the North Atlantic Area*, Princeton, Princeton University Press, 1957, p. 5.

54 Deutsch *et al.*, *Political Community*, p. 118.

55 Deutsch *et al.*, *Political Community*, p. 5.

56 M. Brenner, 'Multilateralism and European security', *Survival*, 1993, vol. 35, no. 2, p. 141.

57 E. Adler and M. Barnett, *Security Communities*, Cambridge, Cambridge University Press, 1998, pp. 34–5.

58 T. Lansford, *Evolution and Devolution: The Dynamics of Sovereignty and Security in post-Cold War Europe*, Aldershot, Ashgate, 2000, p. 39.

59 For more on the role of institutions and organisations see Adler and Barnett, *Security Communities*, pp. 41–3.

60 See B. Møller, *Common Security and Nonoffensive Defence: A Neorealist Perspective*, Boulder, Lynne Rienner, 1992.

61 Collins, *The Security Dilemma*, pp. 45–61.

62 For an introduction to the democratic peace debates see, *inter alia*, C. Layne, 'Kant or cant: the myth of the democratic peace', *International Security*, 1994, vol. 19, no. 2, pp. 5–49 and J. Owen, 'How liberalism produces democratic peace', *International Security*, 1994, vol. 19, no. 2, pp. 87–125.

63 J. L. Gaddis, 'The long peace: elements of stability in the postwar international system', *International Security*, 1986, vol. 10, no. 4, pp. 111–12.

64 R. Keohane and J. Nye, *Power and Interdependence* (2nd edn), Boston, Scott/Foresman, 1989.

65 J. de Wilde, 'Promises of interdependence: risks and opportunities', *Bulletin of Peace Proposals*, 1988, vol. 19, no. 2, p. 163.

66 J. Holmes, *The United States and Europe after the Cold War: A New Alliance?*, Columbia, University of South Carolina Press, 1997, pp. 1–2.

67 J. Joffe, 'Europe's American pacifier', *Foreign Policy*, 1984, no. 54, pp. 68–9.
68 M. Sheridan, 'Holbrooke Aegean jibe angers Foreign Office', *Independent*, 10 February 1996.
69 B. Clark, 'Breakthrough in Greek–Turk relations', *Financial Times*, 9 July 1997.
70 C. Layne, 'Atlanticism without NATO', *Foreign Policy*, 1987, no. 67, p. 24.
71 M. Brenner, *Terms of Engagement: The United States and the European Security Identity*, Westport, Praeger, 1998, p. 63.
72 T. Risse-Kappen, *Cooperation Among Democracies: The European Influence on US Foreign Policy*, Princeton, Princeton University Press, 1995, p. 36.
73 Brenner, *Terms of Engagement*, p. 63.
74 For examples of official US articulations of this view see, *inter alia*, *United States Security Strategy for Europe and NATO*, Washington DC, Office of International Security Affairs, Department of Defense, 1995, p. 1; R. Holbrooke, 'America, a European power', *Foreign Affairs*, 1995, vol. 74, no. 2, pp. 38–51.
75 Adler and Barnett, *Security Communities*, p. 33.
76 R. Cohen and M. Mihalka, *Cooperative Security: New Horizons for International Order*, Garmisch-Partenkirchen, George C. Marshall European Center for Security Studies, 2001, pp. 56–8.
77 P. Dunay, 'Whence the threat to peace in Europe?', in I. Gambles (ed.) *A Lasting Peace in Central Europe? (Chaillot Paper 20)*, Paris, WEU Institute for Security Studies, 1995.
78 See A. Cottey, 'Return to Europe: the transformation of Central and Eastern European security', paper presented to the annual conference of the British International Studies Association, University of Edinburgh, December 2001.
79 In addition to its 1997–9 enlargement round that took in the Czech Republic, Hungary and Poland, NATO's membership further expanded during 2004 to include the three Baltic States, Bulgaria, Romania, Slovakia and Slovenia. At the same time, the EU's membership enlarged to include the Baltic States, the Czech Republic, Hungary, Poland, Slovakia and Slovenia (plus Cyprus and Malta).
80 Dunay, 'Whence the threat to peace in Europe?', p. 41.

2 Dramatis Personae: Russia and NATO since 1991

1 See, *inter alia*, K.-H. Kamp, 'The folly of rapid NATO expansion', *Foreign Policy*, 1995, no. 98, pp. 122–3; J. Killick, 'Small is beautiful: the case against the enlargement of NATO', *RUSI Journal*, 1996, vol. 141, no. 4, p. 58.
2 Article Five of the NATO treaty contains the famous security guarantee: that the members will consider an attack against any one of them as being an attack against them all. The term 'non-Article Five operations' refers, therefore, to any military operation undertaken within a NATO framework for reasons other than responding to a direct attack on one or more of the member states. In NATO treaty terms, the legal basis for such

operations is Article Four, which permits members to 'consult together whenever, in the opinion of any of them, the territorial integrity, political independence or security of any of the Parties is threatened'. See *The North Atlantic Treaty Organisation: Facts and Figures* (hereafter *NATO: Facts and Figures*), Brussels, NATO, 1989, pp. 376–7.

3 *Washington Summit Communiqué*, web text, http://www.nato.int/docu/pr/1999/p99–064e.htm.

4 EU members declared a willingness in principle to do this at their Cologne summit meeting in June 1999, and confirmed their decision in Helsinki six months later. See, respectively, *European Council Declaration on Strengthening the Common European Policy on Security and Defence – June 1999*, web text, http://europa.eu.int/council/off/conclu/june99/annexe_en.htm; *Presidency Conclusions – Helsinki European Council 10 and 11 December 1999*, web text, http://europa.eu.int/council/off/conclu/dec99/dec99_en.htm.

5 For overall discussions of developments during this period see M. A. Smith and G. Timmins, 'The EU: coming of age as a security actor?' and W. Rees, 'The WEU: eliminating the middleman', in Smith and Timmins (eds) *Uncertain Europe: Building a New European Security Order?*, London, Routledge, 2001, chs 5 and 6.

6 On the face of it, there were important developments in the early 2000s. The EU formally took over military operations from NATO in Macedonia in 2003 and Bosnia in 2004. In reality, however, both these operations continued to rely on NATO command and planning structures and it was suggested, therefore, that the actual degree of transition had amounted to little more than 'changing shoulder flashes' on the uniforms of the soldiers involved. See 'NATO's Istanbul summit: Alliance under a cloud', *Strategic Comments*, 2004, vol. 10, no. 5, p. 2, web text, http://www.iiss.org/stratcom. Overall, even by the mid 2000s, it was still not clear that the question of EU relations with NATO had been definitely settled. See 'Let's talk – but where?', *The Economist*, 26 February 2005, p. 48.

7 It should be noted that recently, there has been increasing debate about NATO developing Partnership for Peace type links, or even possibly offering membership, to countries outside Europe. For a good introduction and overview analysis see A. Cottey, 'NATO: globalization or redundancy?', *Contemporary Security Policy*, 2004, vol. 25, no. 3, pp. 391–408.

8 The content of this relationship is based on the 1997 *Charter on a Distinctive Partnership between the North Atlantic Treaty Organization and Ukraine*, web text, http://www.nato.int/docu/basictxt/ukrchrt.htm.

9 On this possibility see A. Browne and J. Page, 'Ukraine bid to join Nato threatens wider rift with Russia', *The Times*, 23 February 2005.

10 Author's interview with a NATO PfP official, June 2004. The author is also grateful to Dmitry Polikanov for discussion of this point.

11 See M. A. Smith, *NATO in the First Decade after the Cold War*, Dordrecht, Kluwer, 2000, ch. 5 for a more detailed discussion of NATO's roles in Bosnia and Kosovo.

12 The Cold War NATO area, specified in Article Six of its treaty, covered the territory of member states in Europe and North America and the islands under their jurisdiction north of the Tropic of Cancer. Territories beyond

this definition, therefore, were regarded during the Cold War years as being 'out-of-area'. See *NATO: Facts and Figures*, p. 377.

13 For a sampling of the speculation see S. Talbott, 'From Prague to Baghdad: NATO at risk', *Foreign Affairs*, 2002, vol. 81, no. 6, pp. 46–57; J. Dempsey, 'If Bush does not make clear that Nato can be involved in critical issues, the alliance will atrophy', *Financial Times*, 20 November 2002; A. Hamilton, 'Nato suffers from a terminal illness, but no one dares kill it off just yet', *Independent*, 22 November 2002.

14 A. Deighton, 'The eleventh of September and beyond: NATO', in Lawrence Freedman (ed.) *Superterrorism: Policy Responses*, Oxford, Blackwell, 2002, pp. 119–20.

15 Quoted in I. Daalder, 'The end of Atlanticism', *Survival*, 2003, vol. 45, no. 2, p. 155.

16 J. Kampfner, *Blair's Wars*, London, Free Press, 2003, p. 117.

17 P. Gordon, 'NATO after 11 September', *Survival*, 2001–02, vol. 43, no. 4, p. 92.

18 Having said this, there were indications, even before September 11, that its member states were beginning to regard the threat posed by international terrorism as an issue that could be brought within NATO's remit. The new strategic concept document, adopted at the Washington summit in April 1999, included terrorism amongst the 'risks of a wider nature' that could 'pose problems for security and stability affecting the Alliance'. See 'The Alliance's Strategic Concept 1999', para. 24, web text, http://www.nato.int/docu/pr/1999/p99–065e.htm.

19 'Statement by the North Atlantic Council' (Press Release (2001)124), web text, http://www.nato.int/docu/pr/2001/p01–124e.htm.

20 Statement by NATO Secretary General, Lord Robertson, 2 October 2001, web text, http://www.nato.int/docu/speech/2001/s011002a.htm. The waters were somewhat muddied by the fact that the Taliban were not recognised as being the legitimate government of Afghanistan by any NATO member. Thus, the basis of the October 2001 statement was the contention that they nevertheless constituted the *de facto* state authorities in Afghanistan.

21 For details of the eight measures see the NATO Secretary-General's Statement to the Press of 4 October 2001, web text, http://www.nato.int/docu/speech/2001/s011004b.htm.

22 D. Brown, ' "The war on terrorism would not be possible without NATO": A Critique', *Contemporary Security Policy*, 2004, vol. 25, no. 3, pp. 22–42.

23 Gordon, 'NATO after 11 September', p. 93.

24 *NATO: Facts and Figures*, p. 377.

25 Gordon, 'NATO after 11 September', p. 93.

26 For a sampling see 'The dangers of a deaf dialogue', *Financial Times*, 10 February 2003; S. Castle, 'Robertson's gamble misfires and the alliance ruptures', *Independent*, 11 February 2003; 'Divisive diplomacy with Europe', *New York Times*, 11 February 2003, web text, http://www.nytimes.com/2003/02/11/.

27 G. Robertson, 'The Omaha milkman today', *RUSI Journal*, 2004, vol. 149, no. 1, p. 44.

28 A. Moravcsik, 'Striking a new transatlantic bargain', *Foreign Affairs*, 2003, vol. 82, no. 4, pp. 78–80.

29 See, *inter alia*, S. Castle, 'France resists US pressure to conduct Nato training in Iraq', *Independent*, 28 July 2004; S. Castle, 'Nato scheme to train Iraqi security forces is blocked', *Independent*, 29 July 2004.

30 For details, therefore, see 'The NATO Training Implementation Mission Arrives in Iraq' (Press Release (26)), web text, http://www.afsouth.nato.int/releases/2004releases/PR_26_04.htm; 'Enhancement of NATO Assistance to Iraq', web text, http://www.nato.int/docu/update/2004/09-september/e0922.htm. In fairness, further enhancements to the training programme in early 2005 were better reported. See, *inter alia*, E. Sciolino, 'NATO agrees on modest plan for training Iraqi forces', *New York Times*, 23 February 2005, web text, http://www.nytimes.com/2005/02/23/, which reported that France had agreed to contribute financially to the NATO in-country training effort.

31 On this latter issue see, *inter alia*, 'Reinforcements needed', *The Economist*, 19 June 2004, pp. 65–6; B. Maddox, 'Security problems in Afghanistan are taking Nato to the brink of failure', *The Times*, 25 June 2004.

32 This is the core underlying issue explored in M. A. Smith (ed.) 'Where is NATO going?' a special issue of *Contemporary Security Policy*, 2004, vol. 25, no. 3.

33 Air Marshal Sir Timothy Garden (now Lord Garden), Sandhurst Defence Forum seminar, 18 May 2004.

34 P. Cornish, 'NATO: the practice and politics of transformation', *International Affairs*, 2004, vol. 80, no. 1, p. 65.

35 Speech at the 41st Munich Conference on Security Policy. Text supplied by the Embassy of the FRG, London.

36 On the origins and evolution of the superpower concept up to the end of the Cold War see K. Aldred and M. A. Smith, *Superpowers in the Post-Cold War Era*, Basingstoke, Macmillan, 1999, ch. 2.

37 A. Kozyrev, 'Russia: a chance for survival', *Foreign Affairs*, 1992, vol. 71, no. 2, pp. 1–16.

38 *Izvestia*, 11 March 1994. Translated in *The Current Digest of the Post-Soviet Press* [hereafter *CDPSP*], 1994, vol. XLVI, no. 10, p. 2.

39 J. Sherr, *Russian Great Power Ideology: Sources and Implications*, Camberley, Conflict Studies Research Centre [hereafter CSRC], 1996.

40 P. Dobriansky, 'Russian foreign policy: promise or peril?', *Washington Quarterly*, 2000, vol. 23, no. 1, p. 141.

41 S. Nunn and A. Stulberg, 'The many faces of modern Russia', *Foreign Affairs*, 2000, vol. 79, no. 2, p. 46. For an extended discussion of the alleged weaknesses of the Russian state see A. Lieven, 'Freedom and anarchy: Russia stumbles toward the twenty-first century', *Washington Quarterly*, 1996, vol. 20, no. 1, pp. 41–58.

42 A. Lynch, 'The realism of Russia's foreign policy', *Europe–Asia Studies*, 2001, vol. 53, no. 1, p. 25.

43 R. Legvold, 'Russia's unformed foreign policy', *Foreign Affairs*, 2001, vol. 80, no. 5, p. 62.

44 On these decisions see, *inter alia*, *Noviye Izvestia*, 28 July 2001. *CDPSP*, 2001, vol. 53, no. 30, p. 19; 'Hope gleams anew', *The Economist*, 3 November 2001, pp. 47–8; *Kommersant*, 6 February 2002. *CDPSP*, 2002, vol. 54, no. 6, p. 17; *Moskovskiye Novosti*, 12–18 February 2002. *CDPSP*, 2002, vol. 54, no. 6, pp. 17–18.

45 For a development of this argument in relation to Cuba see Aldred and Smith, *Superpowers in the Post-Cold War Era*, pp. 124–6.

46 'Putin tells the nation Russia can be rich and strong again', *Johnson's Russia List*, no. 7186, web text, http://www.cdi.org/russia/johnson/7186–1.cfm.

47 The author is grateful to Dmitry Polikanov for these points.

48 'Russia–US Relations and Emerging Threats to National Security', web text, http://wwwc.house.gov/international_relations/109/wal030905.htm. See also *Trud*, 14 October 2003. *CDPSP*, 2003, vol. 55, no. 41, p. 15.

49 S. Stankevich, 'Russia in search of itself', *National Interest*, 1992, vol. 28, pp. 47–51. See also *Nezavisimaya Gazeta*, 28 March 1992. *CDPSP*, 1992, vol. XLIV, no. 13, pp. 1–4. For an assessment of Eurasianist ideas see G. Dijkink, *National Identity and Geopolitical Visions*, London, Routledge, 1996, ch. 8.

50 Kozyrev, 'Russia: a chance for survival', p. 14.

51 For a general overview of the evolution of Russian Asia policy during the early Yeltsin years see C. Harada, *Russia and North-east Asia (Adelphi Paper 310)*, London, IISS, 1997.

52 On Sino-Russian relations see, *inter alia*, R. Menon, 'The strategic convergence between Russia and China', *Survival*, 1997, vol. 39, no. 2, pp. 101–25; E. Bazhanov, 'Russian policy toward China', in P. Shearman (ed.) *Russian Foreign Policy Since 1990*, Boulder, Westview, 1995, ch. 8; S. Prikhodko, 'An invaluable relationship', *Russia in Global Affairs*, 2004, no. 2, web text, http://eng.globalaffairs.ru/numbers/7/529.html.

53 D. Kerr, 'The new Eurasianism: the rise of geopolitics in Russia's foreign policy', *Europe–Asia Studies*, 1995, vol. 47, no. 6, pp. 977–88.

54 V. Baranovsky, 'Russia: a part of Europe or apart from Europe?', *International Affairs*, 2000, vol. 76, no. 3, p. 446. Alexei Arbatov has gone further in asserting that 'strictly speaking, Russia has never existed between Europe and Asia, even geographically. It has always been an east European nation which from the sixteenth century acquired huge territories in northern Asia'. A. Arbatov, 'The transformation of Russia's military doctrine in the aftermath of Kosovo and Chechnya', in G. Gorodetsky (ed.) *Russia between East And West*, London, Frank Cass, 2003, p. 28. For a general discussion of ideas about Russia as a European power, see V. Morozov, 'Inside/Outside: Europe and the Boundaries of Russian Political Community' (PONARS Working Paper 23), web text, http://www.csis.org/ruseura/ponars/workingpapers/023.pdf.

55 J. Matlock, 'Dealing with a Russia in turmoil', *Foreign Affairs*, 1996, vol. 75, no. 3, pp. 45–6.

56 R. Sakwa, 'Putin's foreign policy: transforming "the East"', in Gorodetsky (ed.) *Russia between East And West*, p. 188.

57 See B. Lo, *Vladimir Putin and the Evolution of Russian Foreign Policy*, London, RIIA, 2003; S. Blank, *Towards the Failing State: The Structure of Russian Security Policy*, Camberley, CSRC, 1996 and S. Garnett, 'Russia's illusory ambitions', *Foreign Affairs*, 1997, vol. 76, no. 2, pp. 64–5.

58 K. Kosachev, 'Russian foreign policy vertical', *Russia in Global Affairs*, 2004, no. 3, web text, http://eng.globalaffairs.ru/numbers/8/578.html. See also the critical article by Sergei Karaganov in *Rossiiskaya Gazeta*, 12 January 2005. *CDPSP*, 2005, vol. 57, nos. 1–2, pp. 9–10.

59 Legvold, 'Russia's unformed foreign policy'.
60 See the article by Sergei Rogov in *Nezavisimaya Gazeta*, 31 December 1994. *CDPSP*, 1995, vol. XLVII, no. 1, p. 23. See also Sergei Karaganov in *Rossiiskaya Gazeta*, 12 January 2005.
61 It should be noted, in fairness, that some have seen the apparent failure to choose a firm foreign policy course in a positive light. Lev Klepatskii, for example, has argued that 'for Russia's national interests and security, the optimal choice is balanced openness which allows freedom for manoeuvre in foreign policy. This is especially important as Russia is a country much in demand, a country that each of the poles [of power] wants to have on its own side'. See L. N. Klepatskii, 'The new Russia and the new world order', in Gorodetsky (ed.) *Russia between East And West*, p. 10.
62 S. Covington, *Moscow's Insecurity and Eurasian Instability*, Camberley, CSRC, 1994. In his memoirs, Mikhail Gorbachev claims that he warned Boris Yeltsin that bringing the single Soviet state to an end would make it more difficult to keep the Russian Federation itself together. M. Gorbachev, *Memoirs*, London, Doubleday, 1996, p. 688.
63 This term was 'coined by Russians to distinguish between independent former imperial domains with Russian minorities and the rest of the world'. A. Rubinstein, 'The geopolitical pull on Russia', *Orbis*, 1994, vol. 38, no. 4, p. 571.
64 Aldred and Smith, *Superpowers in the Post-Cold War Era*, p. 109.
65 'Trick or treaty?', *The Economist*, 30 March 1996, pp. 43–9.
66 M. Smith, *Russia and the Near Abroad*, Camberley, CSRC, 1997, pp. 9–10.
67 F. Splidsboel Hansen, 'In the transatlantic gap', *Russia in Global Affairs*, 2004, no. 4, web text, http://eng.globalaffairs.ru/numbers/9/710.html.
68 'Putin tells the nation Russia can be rich and strong again'. See also 'President Putin's Address at the plenary session of ambassadors and permanent representatives of Russia', *Johnson's Russia List*, no. 8290, web text, http://www.cdi.org/russia/johnson/8290-20.cfm.
69 *Izvestia*, 20 July 2004. *CDPSP*, 2004, vol. 56, no. 29, p. 14.
70 Bobo Lo has suggested that Putin has pursued a more consistent and proactive policy towards developing the CIS than did Yeltsin, but without offering much in the way of tangible evidence to back up this claim. See Lo, *Vladimir Putin and the Evolution of Russian Foreign Policy*. For speculation about the developing contours of Putin's policy towards the CIS see I. Kobrinskaya, 'Russian Foreign Policy in the Post-Soviet Space: New Priorities for New Challenges?' (PONARS Policy Memo 332), web text, http://www.csis.org/ruseura/PONARS/policymemos/pm_0332.pdf.
71 R. Pipes, 'Is Russia still an enemy?', *Foreign Affairs*, 1997, vol. 76, no. 5, pp. 71–4. 'Putin's impossible dream', *Johnson's Russia List*, no. 8475, web text, http://www.cdi.org/russia/johnson//8474–16.cfm.
72 D. Simes, 'The return of Russian history', *Foreign Affairs*, 1994, vol. 73, no. 1, p. 81. For Simes' specific arguments with regard to the 2004 presidential elections in Ukraine, see 'Developments in US–Russian Relations', *Johnson's Russia List*, no. 9087, web text, http://www.cdi.org/russia/johnson/9087–23.cfm. See also Rubinstein, 'The geopolitical pull on Russia', p. 573.
73 S. Sestanovich, 'Russia turns the corner', *Foreign Affairs*, 1994, vol. 73, no. 1, pp. 83–98; 'Putin's impossible dream'.

74 On this see, *inter alia*, 'Perplexed by Putin's bet in Ukraine', *Johnson's Russia List*, no. 8435, web text, http://www.cdi.org/russia/johnson/8435-4.cfm; 'Kremlin redefining policy in "Post-Soviet Space"', *Johnson's Russia List*, no. 9054, web text, http://www.cdi.org/russia/johnson/9054-27.cfm.

75 Yekaterina Kuznetsova has described the goal of Russian policy towards the Caucasus region as being the fostering of 'managed instability'. See her 'The near abroad: increasingly far away from Russia', *Russia in Global Affairs*, 2005, no. 1, web text, http://eng.globalaffairs.ru/numbers/10/809.html. See also 'A matter of Russian honour' and 'The hazards of a long, hard freeze', *The Economist*, 21 August 2004, p. 13 and pp. 35–6.

76 M. B. Olcott, 'Sovereignty and the "near abroad"', *Orbis*, 1995, vol. 39, no. 3, pp. 353–67.

77 A. Tsipko, 'A new Russian identity or old Russia's reintegration?', *Security Dialogue*, 1994, vol. 25, no. 4, p. 443.

78 See, *inter alia*, J. Page, 'Moldova turns its back on Russia', *The Times*, 7 March 2005.

79 The author is grateful to Dmitry Polikanov for this point.

80 Quoted in 'Peacekeeping: Russia's special role', *RUSI Newsbrief*, 1993, vol. 13, no. 4, p. 25.

81 'President Putin's Address at the plenary session of ambassadors and permanent representatives of Russia'.

82 See V. Simonov, 'Russia and America search for rules of the game in former Soviet Union', *Johnson's Russia List*, no. 9044, web text, http://www.cdi.org/russia/johnson/9044-24.cfm.

83 A perception of developing competition was especially evident in Russian press commentary at the time of the second round of NATO enlargement in March/April 2004. See, *inter alia*, *Russky Kuryer*, 22 March 2004; *Russky Kuryer*, 25 March 2004; *Trud*, 26 March 2004; *Nezavisimaya Gazeta*, 26 March 2004. All translated in *CDPSP*, 2004, vol. 56, no. 12, pp. 9–10.

84 Another was undoubtedly the numbers of Russians living in these two states. Census figures showed that, in 1989, 30.3 per cent of the population of Estonia and 34 per cent of the population of Latvia were ethnic Russians or Russian speakers. See *Nezavisimaya Gazeta*, 19 July 2001. *CDPSP*, 2001, vol. 53, no. 31, p. 4.

85 See the *Study on NATO Enlargement*, Brussels, NATO, 1995, p. 25.

86 If anything, accession to the EU would present a stiffer challenge in terms of demonstrating respect for minority rights. In June 1993, the EU members, meeting in Copenhagen, had agreed that 'respect for and protection of minorities' would form one of the core criteria that would need to be met before candidate states could be invited to join. See *European Council in Copenhagen 21–22 June 1993: Conclusions of the Presidency*, web text, http://ue.eu.int/ueDocs/cms_Data/docs/pressData/en/ec/72921.pdf.

87 K. Aldred and M. A. Smith, 'Imperial ambition or humanitarian concern? Russia and its "near abroad"', *Journal of Humanitarian Assistance*, web text, http://www.jha.ac/articles/a025.htm.

88 R. Krickus, 'Latvia's "Russian Question"', *Radio Free Europe/Radio Liberty Research Report*, 1993, vol. 2, no. 18, p. 30.

89 *Izvestia*, 10 July 1993. *CDPSP*, 1993, vol. XLV, no. 28, p. 24.

90 Controversies have continued to flare up from time to time over such issues as the official status of the Russian language and Baltic demands for financial compensation for alleged losses incurred during the 'Soviet occupation'. See, *inter alia*, [on language rights] *Kommersant*, 10 July 1999. *CDPSP*, 1999, vol. 51, no. 28, pp. 15–16; *Kommersant*, 16 July 1999. *CDPSP*, 1999, vol. 51, no. 28, p. 16; *Vremya Novostei*, 14 May 2003. *CDPSP*, 2003, vol. 55, no. 19, p. 17. [On compensation claims] *Kommersant*, 28 June 2000. *CDPSP*, 2000, vol. 52, no. 26, p. 16.

91 As evidence that such a diminution has taken place, it is worth noting the decision made by OSCE member states, in December 2001, to close that organisation's missions in both Estonia and Latvia. See *Kommersant*, 21 December 2001. *CDPSP*, 2001, vol. 53, no. 51, pp. 21–2.

92 *Nezavisimaya Gazeta*, 19 July 2001.

93 On this see, *inter alia*, *Nezavisimaya Gazeta*, 6 November 2002. *CDPSP*, 2002, vol. 54, no. 45, pp. 16–17; *Nezavisimaya Gazeta*, 7 March 2003. *CDPSP*, 2003, vol. 55, no. 9, p. 7.

94 See E. Mitrofanova, ' "The Russian world" without borders', *Russia in Global Affairs*, 2004, no.1, web text, http://eng.globalaffairs.ru/numbers/6/512.html.

95 *Nezavisimaya Gazeta*, 19 July 2001.

96 'Fate of the Russian-speaking population of CIS and Baltic countries', *International Affairs* (Moscow), 1995, vol. 6, pp. 113–14.

97 That is, able bodied and skilled workers with some financial assets of their own.

98 *Nezavisimaya Gazeta*, 19 July 2001. See also *Rossiiskaya Gazeta*, 3 August 2001. *CDPSP*, 2001, vol. 53, no. 31, pp. 5–6.

3 Unfulfilled partnerships: Russia and NATO from 'honeymoon' to Kosovo

1 B. Johnson, 'History "turns inside out" as Russia asks to join NATO', *Daily Telegraph*, 21 December 1991.

2 A minority view hinted at a possibly subversive agenda on the part of the Yeltsin government. As *Izvestia* put it: 'to admit Russia into the alliance would mean either to completely reexamine the alliance's aims or to essentially end it in its current form. NATO is not yet prepared to do that'. *Izvestia*, 23 December 1991. *CDSP*, 1991, vol. XLIII, no. 51, p. 22.

3 According to Ira Straus, the Yeltsin government did feel a sense of 'humiliation' at the non-response and attempted to salve its embarrassment by 'putting out the story that its overture to NATO had been a mistranslation'. I. Straus, 'Western common homes and Russian national identities: how Far East can the EU and NATO go, and where does that leave Russia?', *European Security*, 2001, vol. 8, no. 4, p. 19. This story seems to have taken hold in Russia. In 1995, Vladimir Baranovsky referred to 'the well-known typing mistake'. V. Baranovsky, 'Russian foreign policy priorities and Euroatlantic multilateral institutions', *International Spectator*, 1995, vol. XXX, no. 1, p. 38.

4 For examples of the few public statements during 1992 on the issue of whether Russia should join NATO, see the interview with Sergei Blagovolin in *Izvestia*, 22 January 1992. *CDPSP*, 1992, vol. XLIV, no. 3, p. 22 and the article by Alexei Arbatov in *Nezavisimaya Gazeta*, 11 March 1992. *CDPSP*, 1992, vol. XLIV, no. 11, p. 14.

5 A. Kozyrev, 'The new Russia and the Atlantic alliance', *NATO Review*, 1993, vol. 41, no. 1, web text, http://www.nato.int/docu/review/1993/9301-1.htm.

6 English language translation of Shaposhnikov's remarks supplied by Federal News Service, Washington DC, 11 December 1992.

7 English language translation in *BBC Summary of World Broadcasts*, 1993, EE/1778, p. A/8.

8 S. Crow, 'Russian views on an eastward expansion of NATO', *RFE/RL Research Report*, 1993, vol. 2, no. 41, pp. 21–4.

9 Kozyrev, in an interview with the Polish media, had expressed opposition to NATO enlargement into Central Europe. See 'Russia wants neutral Eastern Europe', *RFE/RL News Briefs*, 23–7 August 1993, p. 12.

10 Strobe Talbott, recently appointed as the Clinton administration's chief point man on Russia, has inclined to this view in his memoirs. See S. Talbott, *The Russia Hand: A Memoir of Presidential Diplomacy*, New York, Random House, 2002, pp. 95–7.

11 *Segodnya*, 14 September 1993. *CDPSP*, 1993, vol. XLV, no. 37, pp. 16–17.

12 A. Stent, 'America and Russia: paradoxes of partnership', in A. Motyl *et al.* (eds) *Russia's Engagement with the West*, London, M. E. Sharpe, 2005, p. 275.

13 Not everybody accepted the view that Yeltsin was thus beholden to the military. For a dissenting analysis see B. Taylor, 'Russian civil-military relations after the October uprising', *Survival*, 1994, vol. 36, no. 1, pp. 3–29.

14 'Russian President Boris Yeltsin's letter to US President Bill Clinton', *SIPRI Yearbook 1994*, Oxford, SIPRI/Oxford University Press, 1994, pp. 249–50.

15 *Rossiiskiye Vesti*, 18 November 1993. *CDPSP*, 1993, vol. XLV, no. 46, pp. 11–12.

16 *Newsnight*, 27 October 1993. *Foreign Broadcast Information Service* [hereafter *FBIS*], 1993, FBIS-SOV–93–209, p. 13. See also Baranovsky, 'Russian foreign policy priorities and Euroatlantic multilateral institutions', p. 38; V. Gorskii, 'Problems and prospects of NATO–Russia relationship: the Russian debate', paper prepared under the NATO Euro-Atlantic Partnership Council Fellowships Programme, 1999–2001, pp. 9, 11–12.

17 It has been alleged subsequently that informal approaches were made by senior Russian officials during the early 1990s to ascertain whether Russian membership of NATO was indeed possible. Reportedly, the US responded negatively. Question from Senator Wellstone to Ambassador Thomas Pickering, Senate Foreign Relations Committee Hearings, October 1997. *The Debate on NATO Enlargement*, Washington DC, Committee on Foreign Relations, United States Senate, October/November 1997, web text, http://frwebgate.access.gpo.gov/.

18 'Russian President Boris Yeltsin's letter to US President Bill Clinton', p. 250.
19 *FBIS*, 1993, FBIS-SOV-93–227, p. 6; *Nezavisimaya Gazeta*, 26 November 1993. *CDPSP*, 1993, vol. XLV, no. 47, p. 11.
20 *Komsomolskaya Pravda*, 26 November 1993. *FBIS*, 1993, FBIS-SOV-93–226, p. 10.
21 *Nezavisimaya Gazeta*, 26 November 1993. The translation provided by the Foreign Broadcast Information Service, based on extracts published in *Izvestia*, uses slightly different wording in places but without altering the essential meaning. *Izvestia*, 26 November 1993. *FBIS*, 1993, FBIS-SOV-93–226, pp. 6–8.
22 For a good overview of the nature and substance of PfP, written by a NATO staff member, see N. Williams, 'Partnership for peace: permanent fixture or declining asset?', *Survival*, 1996, vol. 38, no. 1, pp. 98–110.
23 See, *inter alia*, J. Kampfner, 'Yeltsin supports east move by Nato', *Daily Telegraph*, 23 October 1993; 'Your policy or mine?', *The Economist*, 30 October 1993, p. 49; 'Kozyrev views NATO expansion', ITAR-TASS, 3 November 1993. *FBIS*, 1993, FBIS-SOV-93–211, p. 10.
24 Talbott, *The Russia Hand*, p. 115.
25 Quoted in G. Brock and J. Phillips, 'Russian hostility forces retreat on widening of Nato', *The Times*, 2 December 1993.
26 J. Palmer and I. Black, 'East Europeans must wait as Nato favours Russia', *Guardian*, 3 December 1993.
27 *Declaration of the Heads of State and Government (M-1(94)3)*, web text, http://www.nato.int/docu/comm/49–95/c940111a.htm.
28 Senior officer (Lt Gen Leonid Ivashov): *Rossiiskaya Gazeta*, 25 March 1994. *CDPSP*, 1994, vol. XLVI, no. 12, p. 25. Gorbachev: *Nezavisimaya Gazeta*, 13 January 1994. *CDPSP*, 1994, vol. XLVI, no. 2, p. 32.
29 *Nezavisimaya Gazeta*, 18 March 1994. *CDPSP*, 1994, vol. XLVI, no. 11, p. 7.
30 See the articles by Andranik Migranyan in *Nezavisimaya Gazeta*, 15 March 1994. *CDPSP*, 1994, vol. XLVI, no. 11, p. 6 and Vladislav Chernov in *Nezavisimaya Gazeta*, 23 February 1994. *CDPSP*, 1994, vol. XLVI, no. 8, p. 11.
31 *Partnership for Peace: Invitation Document*, web text, http://www.nato.int/docu/basictxt/b940110a.htm.
32 *Nezavisimaya Gazeta*, 23 February 1994.
33 *Nezavisimaya Gazeta*, 2 March 1994. Translated by Federal News Service, Washington DC, 2 March 1994.
34 *Nezavisimaya Gazeta*, 31 March 1994. *CDPSP*, 1994, vol. XLVI, no. 13, pp. 23–4.
35 A. Marshall, 'Moscow to sign deal with NATO', *Independent*, 3 March 1994.
36 J. Headley, 'Sarajevo, February 1994: the first Russia–NATO crisis of the post-Cold War era', *Review of International Studies*, 2003, vol. 29, no. 2, p. 209.
37 *Izvestia*, 24 February 1994. *CDPSP*, 1994, vol. XLVI, no. 8, p. 29.
38 M. Bowker, 'Russian policy toward Central and Eastern Europe', in P. Shearman (ed.) *Russian Foreign Policy since 1990*, Boulder, Westview, 1995, p. 88.

39 *Segodnya*, 15 April 1994. *CDPSP*, 1994, vol. XLVI, no. 15, p. 9.

40 A. Philps, 'Nato deal is spurned by angry Russia', *Daily Telegraph*, 15 April 1994; A. Marshall, 'Moscow pulls out of peace pact with Nato', *Independent*, 16 April 1994.

41 Baranovsky, 'Russian foreign policy priorities and Euroatlantic multilateral institutions', p. 46.

42 A. Marshall, 'Nato moves to ease Moscow fears after Bosnia air-strikes', *Independent*, 19 April 1994.

43 Press Communiqué M-NAC-1(94)06, web text, http://www.nato.int/docu/comm/49–95/c940609b.htm.

44 The document was so named because NATO members had not been prepared to sign a legally binding charter or treaty. See *Summary of Conclusions*, web text, http://www.nato.int/docu/comm/49–95/c940622a.htm.

45 There are two steps for eastern participants in joining PfP. The first, common to all, involves signing the Framework Document. This is a short statement of basic principles and objectives, as agreed at the 1994 Brussels summit. Having done this, partners are free to develop Individual Partnership Programmes with NATO and its member states. These detail the actual military co-operation, and are more extensive for some partners than for others. In June 1994, Russia took the first step.

46 Kozyrev's critics in Russia pointed out that the signing had taken place on the anniversary of Hitler's attack on the Soviet Union in 1941. See *Pravda*, 23 June 1994. *CDPSP*, 1994, vol. XLVI, no. 25, p. 23.

47 Talbott, *The Russia Hand*, p. 123.

48 A. Marshall, 'Russians sign up for closer Nato links', *Independent*, 23 June 1994.

49 Press Communiqué M-NAC-2(94)116, web text, http://www.nato.int/docu/comm/49–95/c941201a.htm.

50 *Segodnya*, 3 December 1994. *CDPSP*, 1994, vol. XLVI, no. 48, p. 18.

51 I. Maksimychev, 'Russia in Europe', *International Affairs* (Moscow), 1998, vol. 44, no. 3, p. 30.

52 'The Visegrad states: crossroads to change in the heart of Europe', *Department of State Dispatch*, 1994, vol. 5, supp. 1, web text, http://dosfan.lib.uic.edu/ERC/briefing/dispatch/1994/html/Dispatchv5sup1.html.

53 'President Clinton Address to the Polish Parliament', *Department of State Dispatch*, 1994, vol. 5, no. 31, web text, http://dosfan.lib.uic.edu/ERC/briefing/1994/html/Dispatchv5no31.html.

54 *BBC Summary of World Broadcasts*, 1994, EE/2043, p. A/7.

55 M. A. Smith and G. Timmins, *Building a Bigger Europe: EU and NATO Enlargement in Comparative Perspective*, Aldershot, Ashgate, 2000.

56 *Remarks by the President in Live Telecast to Russian People*. Washington DC, White House Office of the Press Secretary, 1994.

57 Z. Brzezinski, 'The premature partnership', *Foreign Affairs*, 1994, vol. 73, no. 2, p. 70.

58 J. Morrison, 'Yalta II or Realpolitik?', *Washington Times*, 6 September 1994.

59 *Izvestia*, 28 September 1994. *CDPSP*, 1994, vol. XLVI, no. 39, pp. 25–6. For commentary see *Segodnya*, 30 September 1994. *CDPSP*, 1994, vol. XLVI, no. 39, pp. 4–5.

60 J. Bone, 'US and Russia carve out "spheres of influence"', *The Times*, 27 September 1994; *Krasnaya Zvezda*, 1 October 1994. *CDPSP*, 1994, vol. XLVI, no. 40, p. 24.

61 B. Clark and V. Marsh, 'Yeltsin denounces Nato plans to expand eastwards', *Financial Times*, 6 December 1994.

62 Yeltsin: B. Clark, 'Yeltsin calls for talks with Clinton in Moscow', *Financial Times*, 17 March 1995; Kozyrev: M. Sheridan, 'Russia warns West against Nato growth', *Independent*, 21 March 1995.

63 A. Philps, 'Russia will tear up arms pact if Nato is expanded', *Daily Telegraph*, 4 April 1995.

64 A. Arbatov, 'NATO and Russia', *Security Dialogue*, 1995, vol. 26, no. 2, p. 146. See also A. Lieven, 'Russian opposition to NATO expansion', *The World Today*, 1995, vol. 51, no. 10, p. 199.

65 'European security architecture needs Russia to be complete', *Official Text*, London, US Information Service, US Embassy, 1995, p. 7.

66 'Areas for Pursuance of a Broad, Enhanced NATO/Russia Dialogue and Cooperation', web text,
http://www.nato.int/docu/comm/49–95/c950531a.htm.

67 A. Pierre and D. Trenin, 'Developing NATO–Russian relations', *Survival*, 1997, vol. 39, no. 1, p. 7.

68 A. Adamishin, 'Help us with a freeze on Nato', *The European*, 2–8 June 1995.

69 Talbott, *The Russia Hand*, pp. 156, 161–2. See also *Segodnya*, 9 December 1994. *CDPSP*, 1994, vol. XLVI, no. 49, p. 13; P. Almond, 'Russia agrees to military pact with the West', *Daily Telegraph*, 1 June 1995.

70 On this see 'The Mamedov visit to Washington', *Strategic Forum*, 1995, no. 34, p. 3; C. Goldsmith, 'Russia indicates terms to accept larger NATO', *Wall Street Journal*, 13 March 1995. According to *Moskovskiye Novosti*, this initiative had resulted in Kozyrev being 'called on the carpet' by the President. *Moskovskiye Novosti*, 19–26 March 1995. *CDPSP*, 1995, vol. XLVII, no. 11, pp. 25–6.

71 See, *inter alia*, B. Clark, 'Solana seeks to win over Russia', *Financial Times*, 11 January 1996.

72 See, *inter alia*, J. Thornhill, 'Russia hints at Nato compromise', *Financial Times*, 12 March 1996; A. Gimson, 'Russia eases tone on Nato expansion', *Daily Telegraph*, 5 June 1996; I. Karacs, 'Russians pull back from confrontation with Nato', *Independent*, 5 June 1996; *Kommersant-Daily*, 14–15 August 1996. *CDPSP*, 1996, vol. XLVIII, no. 33, pp. 23–4.

73 'A New Atlantic community for the 21st century', *Department of State Dispatch*, 1996, vol. 7, no. 37, web text, http://dosfan.lib.uic.edu/ERC/briefing/dispatch/1996/html/Dispatchv7no37.html.

74 'Perry speaks on security relationship with Russia', *American Forces Information Service News Articles*, web text,
http://www.defenselink.mil/news/Oct1996/n10301996_9610301.html.

75 Press Communiqué M-NAC-2(96)165, web text,
http://www.nato.int/docu/pr/1996/p96–165e.htm.

76 Quoted in G. de Jonquières, 'Russia softens stance on Nato growth', *Financial Times*, 4 February 1997.

77 C. Freeland, 'Yeltsin eyes compromise on Nato expansion', *Financial Times*, 24 February 1997.

78 See, *inter alia*, C. Scott, 'Yeltsin climbs down under covering fire of summit laughter', *Independent*, 23 March 1997; 'Sops for Russia', *The Economist*, 29 March 1997, p. 48.
79 *Rossiiskaya Gazeta*, 27 March 1997. *CDPSP*, 1997, vol. XLIX, no. 13, pp. 26–7; J. Goldgeier and M. McFaul, *Power and Purpose: US Policy toward Russia after the Cold War*, Washington DC, Brookings, 2003, pp. 206–8; Talbott, *The Russia Hand*, pp. 237–43.
80 Statement by the North Atlantic Council (Press Release (97)27), web text, http://www.nato.int/docu/pr/1997/p97–027e.htm.
81 See J. Borawski, *The NATO–Russia Founding Act (ISIS Briefing Paper 12)*, web text, http://www.isis-europe.org/isiseu/english/no12.html.
82 N. Afanasievskii, 'On the NATO–Russia Founding Act', *International Affairs* (Moscow), 1997, vol. 43, no. 4, pp. 159ff.
83 'Javier Solana, NATO's master-builder', *The Economist*, 17 October 1998, p. 60.
84 On this see Talbott, *The Russia Hand*, ch. 9; Goldgeier and McFaul, *Power and Purpose*, p. 203; 'A new European order', *The Economist*, 17 May 1997, p. 43.
85 *Founding Act on Mutual Relations, Cooperation and Security between NATO and the Russian Federation*, web text, http://www.nato.int/docu/basictxt/fndact-a.htm.
86 This phrase was attributed to the then German Foreign Minister, Klaus Kinkel. See 'Wooing a bear', *The Economist*, 14 December 1996, p. 47.
87 *Izvestia*, 28 May 1997. *CDPSP*, 1997, vol. XLIX, no. 21, p. 5.
88 *Nezavisimaya Gazeta*, 27 May 1997. *CDPSP*, 1997, vol. XLIX, no. 22, pp. 10–11.
89 Quoted in *Russia and European Security* (Document A/1722), Paris, Assembly of the Western European Union, 2000, web text, http://www.assembly-weu.org/en/documents/sessions_ordinaires/rpt/2000/1722.html. See also *Segodnya*, 16 May 1997. *CDPSP*, 1997, vol. XLIX, no 20, pp. 2–4.
90 Testimony of Hon. Henry Kissinger, *The Debate on NATO Enlargement*. See also K.-H. Kamp, 'The NATO–Russia Founding Act: Trojan Horse or milestone of reconciliation?', *Aussenpolitik*, 1997, no. 4, pp. 320–1.
91 Following the successful conclusion of the Solana–Primakov negotiations, an unnamed NATO 'source' was quoted as saying that 'we have . . . told the Russians that this agreement is just the beginning and that, as the relationship improves, their role could become even more significant'. See M. Evans, 'Deal grants Russians unique Nato access while denying veto', *The Times*, 17 May 1997.
92 Ambassador Pickering response to question from Senator Hagel, *The Debate on NATO Enlargement*.
93 Kamp, 'The NATO–Russia Founding Act', p. 324.
94 *NATO–Russia Relations and Next Steps for NATO Enlargement* (Document AS277PCED-E), Brussels, NATO Parliamentary Assembly, 1999, web text, http://www.nato-pa.int/publications/comrep/1999/as277pced-e.html.
95 Col. Gen. L. Ivashov, 'Russia–NATO: matters of cooperation', *International Affairs* (Moscow), 1998, vol. 44, no. 6, p. 113.

96 *Segodnya*, 10 December 1998. *CDPSP*, 1998, vol. 50, no. 49, p. 19.
97 See, *inter alia*, K.-P. Klaiber, 'The NATO–Russia relationship a year after Paris', *NATO Review*, 1998, vol. 46, no. 3, pp. 16–19.
98 *Rossiiskaya Gazeta*, 26 March 1999. *CDPSP*, 1998 [*sic*], vol. 51, no. 12, pp. 2–3.
99 *Founding Act*, Part I.
100 Goldgeier and McFaul, *Power and Purpose*, p. 253.
101 P. Trenin-Straussov, *The NATO–Russia Permanent Joint Council in 1997–1999: Anatomy of a Failure*, Berlin, Berlin Information Center for Transatlantic Security, 1999, web text, http://www.bits.de/public/researchnote/rn99–1.htm.
102 WEU Assembly, *Russia and European Security*.
103 Trenin-Straussov, *The NATO–Russia Permanent Joint Council in 1997–1999*.
104 NATO Parliamentary Assembly, *NATO–Russia Relations*. See also Y. Davydov, 'Should Russia Join NATO?', paper prepared under the NATO Euro-Atlantic Partnership Council Fellowships programme, 1998–2000, pp. 12–13, 20–1.
105 D. Trenin, 'Russia–NATO relations: Time to pick up the pieces', *NATO Review*, 2000, vol. 48, no. 1, p. 21.

4 The Kosovo crisis

1 V. Baranovsky, 'Russia: a part of Europe or apart from Europe?', *International Affairs*, 2000, vol. 76, no. 3, p. 455; M. Smith, *Russia and the Far Abroad 2000*, Camberley, CSRC, 2000, p. 3. See also S. Talbott, *The Russia Hand: A Memoir of Presidential Diplomacy*, New York, Random House, 2002, p. 297; J. Goldgeier and M. McFaul, *Power and Purpose: US Policy toward Russia after the Cold War*, Washington DC, Brookings, 2003, p. 247.
2 Resolution 1160 (1998), web text, http://www.un.org/Docs/scres/1998/sres1160.htm.
3 *Kommersant-Daily*, 3 April 1998. *CDPSP*, 1998, vol. 50, no. 14, p. 23.
4 Resolution 1199 (1998), web text, http://www.un.org/Docs/scres/1998/sres1199.htm.
5 *Izvestia*, 25 September 1998. *CDPSP*, 1998, vol. 50, no. 39, pp. 19–20.
6 C. Guicherd, 'International Law and the War in Kosovo', *Survival*, 1999, vol. 41, no. 2, pp. 26–7.
7 In the US case, Strobe Talbott writes that 'as President Clinton thought about the coming showdown with Milosevic, he attached special importance to maintaining some form of partnership with the Russians'. Talbott, *The Russia Hand*, p. 299.
8 'Joint Statement by Secretary of State Albright and Russian Foreign Minister Ivanov, Moscow, 26 January 1999', reprinted in M. Weller (ed.) *The Crisis in Kosovo 1989–1999*, Cambridge, Documents and Analysis Publishing, 1999, p. 414.
9 For general assessments of this final attempt to settle the crisis by diplomatic means see M. Weller, 'The Rambouillet conference on Kosovo',

International Affairs, 1999, vol. 75, no. 2, pp. 211–51; A. Bellamy, 'Lessons unlearned: why coercive diplomacy failed at Rambouillet', *International Peacekeeping*, 2000, vol. 7, no. 2, pp. 95–114.

10 Weller, 'The Rambouillet conference on Kosovo', p. 251. See also *Nezavisimaya Gazeta*, 23 February 1999. *CDPSP*, 1998 [*sic*], vol. 51, no. 8, p. 18.

11 See *Segodnya*, 17 March 1999. *CDPSP*, 1998 [*sic*], vol. 51, no. 11, p. 20.

12 T. Judah, *Kosovo: War and Revenge*, New Haven, Yale University Press, 2000, p. 198; Weller, 'The Rambouillet conference on Kosovo', p. 251.

13 *Izvestia*, 7 October 1998. *CDPSP*, 1998, vol. 50, no. 40, p. 14.

14 Independent International Commission on Kosovo, *Kosovo Report*, Oxford, Oxford University Press, 2000, p. 161.

15 The Communist leader, Gennady Zyuganov, had called for this on the day after air operations were launched. *Sovetskaya Rossia*, 27 March 1999. *CDPSP*, 1999, vol. 51, no. 12, p. 5.

16 *Vremya MN*, 26 March 1999. *CDPSP*, 1999, vol. 51, no. 12, pp. 3–4.

17 M. Smith, *Russian Thinking on European Security after Kosovo*, Camberley, Conflict Studies Research Centre, 1999, p. 6.

18 Quoted in D. Lynch, ' "Walking the tightrope": The Kosovo conflict and Russia in European security, 1998–August 1999', *European Security*, 1999, vol. 8, no. 4, p. 70.

19 *Izvestia*, 25 March 1999. *CDPSP*, 1999, vol. 51, no. 12, p. 9.

20 *Rossiiskaya Gazeta*, 26 March 1999. *CDPSP*, 1999, vol. 51, no. 12, p. 3.

21 On this see M. Smith, *Contemporary Russian Perceptions of Euro-Atlanticism*, Camberley, Conflict Studies Research Centre, 2002.

22 *Rossiiskaya Gazeta*, 31 March 1999. *CDPSP*, 1999, vol. 51, no. 13, p. 2.

23 *Trud*, 8 April 1999. *CDPSP*, 1999, vol. 51, no. 14, p. 5. See also B. Posen, 'The war for Kosovo', *International Security*, 2000, vol. 24, no. 4, p. 67.

24 V. Baranovsky, 'Russia's interests are too important', *International Affairs* (Moscow), 1999, vol. 45, no. 3, p. 11.

25 *Nezavisimaya Gazeta*, 15 April 1999. *CDPSP*, 1999, vol. 51, no. 15, p. 12.

26 'The situation in and around Kosovo' (Press Release M-NAC-1(99)51), web text, http://www.nato.int/docu/pr/1999/p99–051e.htm.

27 'Kosovo Peace Plan', web text, http://www.basicint.org/peaceplan.htm.

28 I. Daalder and M. O'Hanlon, *Winning Ugly: NATO's War to Save Kosovo*, Washington DC, Brookings, 2000, pp. 165–6; Posen, 'The war for Kosovo', p. 67.

29 Statement by the Chairman on the conclusion of the meeting of the G8 Foreign Ministers on the Petersberg, web text, http://www.g7.utoronto.ca/g7/foreign/fm990506.htm.

30 Lynch, ' "Walking the tightrope" ', pp. 75–6.

31 Transcript of interview with Talbott in *Frontline: War in Europe*, web text, http://www.pbs.org/wgbh/pages/frontline/shows/kosovo/interviews/talbott.html.

32 E. Yesson, 'NATO and Russia in Kosovo', *RUSI Journal*, 1999, vol. 144, no. 4, p. 24.

33 Transcript of interview with Chernomyrdin in *Frontline: War in Europe*, web text, http://www.pbs.org/wgbh/pages/frontline/shows/kosovo/interviews/ chernomyrdin.html.

34 Talbott interview, *Frontline: War in Europe*. See also Daalder and O'Hanlon, *Winning Ugly*, p. 169.
35 Interview with Ahtisaari in 'Lessons of the Kosovo crisis', *International Affairs* (Moscow), 1999, vol. 45, no. 4, p. 14.
36 Talbott interview, *Frontline: War in Europe*.
37 For such arguments see, *inter alia*, Smith, *Russian Thinking on European Security after Kosovo*, pp. 7–9; *Izvestia*, 7 May 1999. *CDPSP*, 1999, vol. 51, no. 18, p. 4.
38 Resolution 1244 (1999), web text, http://www.un.org/Docs/scres/1999/99sc1244.htm.
39 Daalder and O'Hanlon, *Winning Ugly*, pp. 172–3.
40 Daalder and O'Hanlon, *Winning Ugly*, p. 118.
41 For the view that the move was, in fact, ordered by 'rogue' elements in the Russian military, see Talbott, *The Russia Hand*, ch. 13; Goldgeier and McFaul, *Power and Purpose*, pp. 262–3.
42 *Segodnya*, 14 June 1999. *CDPSP*, 1999, vol. 51, no. 24, p. 1.
43 *Izvestia*, 15 June 1999. *CDPSP*, 1999, vol. 51, no. 24, p. 3; *Slovo*, 16–17 June 1999. *CDPSP*, 1999, vol. 51, no. 24, p. 5.
44 The author is grateful to Dmitry Polikanov for this point. See also S. Cross, 'Russia and NATO toward the 21st century: conflicts and peacekeeping in Bosnia-Herzegovina and Kosovo', paper prepared under the NATO Euro-Atlantic Partnership Council Fellowships programme, 1999–2001, pp. 16–17.
45 Gen. Wesley K. Clark, *Waging Modern War: Bosnia, Kosovo and the Future of Combat*, Oxford, Public Affairs, 2001, ch. 15.
46 Clark, *Waging Modern War*, p. 387.
47 For the text of the subsequent agreement and associated attachments see 'Agreed points on Russian participation in KFOR', web text, http://www.nato.int/kfor/resources/documents/helsinki.htm.
48 *Vremya MN*, 5 July 1999. *CDPSP*, 1999, vol. 51, no. 27, p. 8.

5 The new millennium: September 11, Iraq and the NATO–Russia Council

1 I. Daalder and M. O'Hanlon, *Winning Ugly: NATO's War to Save Kosovo*, Washington DC, Brookings, 2000, p. 198.
2 'Russia and European Security' (Document A/1722), Paris, Assembly of the Western European Union, 2000, web text, http://www.assembly-weu.org/en/documents/sessions_ordinaires/rpt/2000/1722.html. See also *Kommersant*, 24 July 1999. *CDPSP*, 1999, vol. 51, no. 30, p. 19.
3 *Trud*, 8 September 1999. *CDPSP*, 1999, vol. 51, no. 36, p. 20; M. Binyon, 'Envoy is sent back to NATO', *The Times*, 2 September 1999.
4 O. Antonenko, 'Russia, NATO and European security after Kosovo', *Survival*, 1999–2000, vol. 41, no. 4, p. 137.
5 See, *inter alia*, *Kommersant*, 24 July 1999.
6 Ivanov: *Nezavisimaya Gazeta*, 12 October 1999. *CDPSP*, 1999, vol. 51, no. 41, p. 3; Primakov: E. MacAskill, 'NATO and Russia re-establish ties as tensions ease', *Guardian*, 17 February 2000.

7 Joint Statement on the occasion of the visit of the Secretary General of NATO, Lord Robertson, in Moscow on 16 February 2000, web text, http://www.nato.int/docu/pr/2000/p000216e.htm. For contemporary commentary and analysis see P. Beauplet, 'Springtime for Russia and NATO', *Jane's Defence Weekly*, 1 March 2000, p. 21.

8 Quoted in MacAskill, 'NATO and Russia re-establish ties as tensions ease'.

9 *Segodnya*, 17 February 2000. *CDPSP*, 2000, vol. 52, no. 7, p. 19. See also V. Kozin, 'The Kremlin and NATO: prospects for interaction', *International Affairs* (Moscow), 2000, vol. 46, no. 3, pp. 17–18.

10 Kozin, 'The Kremlin and NATO', pp. 18–19. The issues discussed at PJC meetings since 1997 are summarised in *NATO–Russia Permanent Joint Council*, Brussels, NATO Parliamentary Assembly, web text, http://www.nato-pa.int/publications/special/pjc.html.

11 See, *inter alia*, *Izvestia*, 7 March 2000. *CDPSP*, 2000, vol. 52, no. 10, p. 5; *Kommersant*, 7 March 2000. *CDPSP*, 2000, vol. 52, no. 10, p. 5; 'The fist unclenched', *The Times*, 6 March 2000.

12 Statement by Lord Robertson, NATO Secretary General, on Acting President Putin's interview with the BBC (Press Release (2000) 023), web text, http://www.nato.int/docu/pr/2000/p00–023e.htm.

13 Quoted in G. Whittell, 'Putin uses Frost to begin thaw with West', *The Times*, 6 March 2000.

14 G. Whittell and M. Evans, 'Putin "redeploys nuclear arms on Baltic coast"', *The Times*, 4 January 2001. See also *Moskovskiye Novosti*, 18–24 January 2000. *CDPSP*, 2000, vol. 52, no. 4, pp. 19–20.

15 A. Lagnado and G. Whittell, 'Putin composure slips over Chechnya claim', *The Times*, 19 July 2001. See also Kozin, 'The Kremlin and NATO', p. 12.

16 For a balanced overview see A. Zagorski, 'Great expectations', *NATO Review*, 2001, vol. 49, no. 1, pp. 24–7.

17 H. Plater-Zyberk and A. Aldis, *Russia's Reaction to the American Tragedy*, Camberley, CSRC, 2001, p. 3.

18 R. Boyes, 'Putin is impatient for Nato welcome', *The Times*, 27 September 2001; 'Russia: Putin backs antiterrorism effort, seeks to join NATO', *RFE/RL*, web text,
http://www.rferl.org/nca/features/2001/09/260926122945.asp.

19 K. Knox, 'Russia: will war on terrorism boost Russia's chances of joining NATO?', *RFE/RL*, web text,
http://www.rferl.org/nca/features/2001/10/03102001123515.asp.

20 L. Hill, 'NATO fails to warm to Putin', *Jane's Defence Weekly*, 7 November 2001, p. 21.

21 'Russia: Putin says not interested in NATO membership', *RFE/RL*, web text, http://www.rferl.org/nca/features/2001/11/221122084257.asp.

22 See, *inter alia*, T. Ambrosio, 'From balancer to ally? Russo-American relations in the wake of 11 September', *Contemporary Security Policy*, 2003, vol. 24, no. 2, p. 2; D. Treisman, 'Russia renewed?', *Foreign Affairs*, 2002, vol. 81, no. 6, p. 68.

23 For examples see, *inter alia*, O. Antonenko, 'Putin's gamble', *Survival*, 2001–02, vol. 43, no. 4, pp. 51, 57; A. Stent and L. Shevtsova, 'America, Russia and Europe: a realignment?', *Survival*, 2002–03, vol. 44, no. 4, p. 123; L. Selezneva, 'Post-Soviet Russian foreign policy: between doctrine

and pragmatism', in R. Fawn (ed.) *Realignments in Russian Foreign Policy*, London, Frank Cass, 2003, pp. 23ff.

24 Quoted in C. Bremner, 'Russia and West to work more closely on security', *The Times*, 4 October 2001.

25 *Kommersant*, 28 September 2001. *CDPSP*, 2001, vol. 53, no. 39, pp. 6–7.

26 *New Developments in Russia, Belarus and Ukraine* (Document A/1761), Paris, Assembly of the Western European Union, 2001, web text, http://www.assemblee-ueo.org/en/documents/sessions_ordinaires/rpt/2001/1761.html.

27 See, *inter alia*, *Noviye Izvestia*, 20 November 2001. *CDPSP*, 2001, vol. 53, no. 47, pp. 20–1; M. Evans, 'Blair plans wider role for Russia with Nato', *The Times*, 17 November 2001.

28 Press Conference with NATO Secretary General, Lord Robertson, 22 November 2001, web text, http://www.nato.int/docu/speech/2001/s011122b.htm.

29 'A New Quality in the NATO–Russia Relationship'. Speech by NATO Secretary General, Lord Robertson at the Diplomatic Academy, 22 November 2001, web text, http://www.nato.int/docu/speech/2001/s011122a.htm.

30 Press Conference with NATO Secretary General, Lord Robertson. See note 28.

31 *Noviye Izvestia*, 20 November 2001. *CDPSP*, 2001, vol. 53, no. 47, p. 21.

32 Press Communiqué M-NAC-2(2001)158, web text, http://www.nato.int/docu/pr/2001/p01–158e.htm.

33 *Izvestia*, 12 January 2002. *CDPSP*, 2002, vol. 54, no. 2, p. 18.

34 *Vremya MN*, 19 January 2002. *CDPSP*, 2002, vol. 54, no. 3, p. 3. See also I. Kobrinskaya, 'The Multispeed Commonwealth', *Russia in Global Affairs*, 2004, no. 1, web text, http://eng.globalaffairs.ru/numbers/6/509.html.

35 See K. Bosworth, 'The Effect of 11th September on Russia–NATO Relations'. Paper presented to the annual conference of the British Association for Slavonic and East European Studies, University of Cambridge, April 2002, pp. 12–13.

36 J. Dempsey, 'Nato woos Russia with offer of closer relations', *Financial Times*, 25 February 2002. This article was subsequently criticised within NATO circles as being 'highly inaccurate'. See *A Summary of the Meetings at NATO and SHAPE of the Joint Monitoring Group on the NATO–Russia Founding Act*, Brussels, NATO Parliamentary Assembly, 2002, web text, http://www.nato-pa.int/publications/special/av076-jmg-rus.html. For corroboration of the key points made in the *FT* article see K. Knox, 'NATO: Alliance mulls details of larger role for Russia', *RFE/RL*, web text, http://www.rferl.org/nca/features/2002/02/27022002095238.asp.

37 *A Summary of the Meetings at NATO and SHAPE*; see note 36.

38 M. Binyon, 'Russia "will stand by coalition even if Iraq is attacked"', *The Times*, 15 March 2002.

39 K. Knox, 'NATO: Robertson says talks with Russia are on schedule', *RFE/RL*, web text, http://www.rferl.org/nca/features/2002/03/21032002085203.asp.

40 The Reykjavik communiqué simply stated that the NRC would be created and in it 'NATO member states and Russia will work as equal partners in areas of common interest, while preserving NATO's prerogative to act independently'. See *M-NAC-1(2002)59*, web text, http://www.nato.int/docu/pr/2002/p02–059e.htm.

41 Bobo Lo has referred to the NRC as being 'perhaps the most impressive of all Putin's achievements in the security sphere'. B. Lo, *Vladimir Putin and the Evolution of Russian Foreign Policy*, London, RIIA, 2003, p. 125.

42 'The new alliance', *The Times*, 15 May 2002.

43 I. Traynor, 'Russia and Nato reach historic deal', *Guardian*, 15 May 2002.

44 I. Straus, 'The new NATO–Russia Council in context: one step in a series, many more to come', *Johnson's Russia List*, no. 6276, web text, http://www.cdi.org/russia/johnson/6276–9.cfm. See also *Noviye Izvestia*, 16 May 2002. *CDPSP*, 2002, vol. 54, no. 20, p. 5; *Trud*, 30 May 2002. *CDPSP*, 2002, vol. 54, no. 22, p. 4.

45 For differing views on what NATO members had agreed on this score see M. Evans, 'Russia to move into Nato HQ', *The Times*, 15 May 2002 and J. Dempsey and R. Wolffe, 'In from the cold', *Financial Times*, 15 May 2002.

46 K. Knox, 'NATO: Robertson says talks with Russia are on schedule'; see note 39.

47 Statement by Ian Brzezinski, Deputy Assistant Secretary of Defense for European and NATO Affairs, House Subcommittee on Europe, Committee on International Relations, June 19 2002, web text, http://www.house.gov/international_relations/brze0619.htm.

48 'NATO–Russia Relations: a new quality.' Declaration by Heads of State and Government of NATO Member States and the Russian Federation, web text, http://www.nato.int/docu/basictxt/b020528e.htm.

49 R. Owen and M. Evans, 'Nato and Russia sign deal to end 50 years of fear', *The Times*, 29 May 2002.

50 *Founding Act on Mutual Relations, Cooperation and Security between NATO and the Russian Federation*, web text, http://www.nato.int/docu/basictxt/fndact-a.htm.

51 'Remarks by NATO Secretary General, Lord Robertson at the NATO–Russia Summit', web text, http://www.nato.int/docu/speech/2002/s020528b.htm.

52 'Follies in the forum', *Guardian*, 29 May 2002.

53 'Russian media critical of new pact with NATO', *Johnson's Russia List*, no. 6276, web text, http://www.cdi.org/russia/johnson/6276–2.cfm.

54 See, *inter alia*, 'Russia: head of mission in Moscow discusses new joint council', *Johnson's Russia List*, no. 6336, web text, http://www.cdi.org/russia/johnson/6336.txt.

55 Quoted in K. Knox, 'NATO: Alliance mulls details of larger role for Russia'; see note 36.

56 V. Gorskii, 'Problems and prospects of NATO–Russia relationship: the Russian debate', paper prepared under the NATO Euro-Atlantic Partnership Council Fellowships Programme, 1999–2001, pp. 43–4; L. Tomé, 'Russia and NATO's enlargement', paper prepared under the NATO Research Fellowship Programme, 1998–2000, p. 25.

57 *Nezavisimaya Gazeta*, 26 September 2002. *CDPSP*, 2002, vol. 54, no. 39,

p. 16; *Vremya Novostei*, 21 November 2002. *CDPSP*, 2002, vol. 54, no. 47, pp. 4–5.

58 'A New Russian Revolution: Partnership with NATO' web text, http://www.nato.int/docu/speech/2002/s021213a.htm.

59 *Kommersant*, 21 August 2002. *CDPSP*, 2002, vol. 54, no. 34, p. 16.

60 *Vremya Novostei*, 22 November 2002. *CDPSP*, 2002, vol. 54, no. 47, p. 1.

61 *Izvestia*, 4 February 2003. *CDPSP*, 2003, vol. 55, no. 5, p. 4; *Noviye Izvestia*, 5 February 2003. *CDPSP*, 2003, vol. 55, no. 5, p. 4.

62 *Vremya Novostei*, 31 January 2003. *CDPSP*, 2003, vol. 55, no. 4, p. 4.

63 M. Smith, *Russia and the Middle East*, Camberley, CSRC, 2002, p. 3.

64 On this see, *inter alia*, R. Watson, 'Putin and Bush start to patch up differences', *The Times*, 2 June 2003.

65 Press Conference by NATO Secretary General, Lord Robertson following the meeting of the NATO–Russia Council, web text, http://www.nato.int/docu/speech/2003/s030513a.htm.

66 'The Reflections of the US Ambassador to Moscow on the US-Russian Partnership', *Johnson's Russia List*, no. 7017, web text, http://www.cdi.org/russia/johnson/7017-2.cfm.

67 Quoted in M. Binyon, 'Kremlin sees fruits of its foreign policy', *The Times*, 21 November 2002.

68 A. Grushko, 'On the new quality of Russia–NATO relations', *International Affairs* (Moscow), 2002, vol. 48, no. 5, p. 27.

69 Press Conference by NATO Secretary General, Lord Robertson and Russian Defence Minister Sergei Ivanov, web text, http://www.nato.int/docu/speech/2003/s030513c.htm.

70 See: (Lord Robertson) 'A Time for Action: breathing life into the NATO–Russia partnership', web text, http://www.nato.int/docu/articles/2002/a021010a.htm; (UK Foreign Secretary Jack Straw) 'Minutes of Evidence taken before the Foreign Affairs Committee Thursday 14 November 2002', para. 85, web text, http://www.publications.parliament.uk/pa/cm200203/cmselect/cmfaff/66-i/2111401.htm; (Alexander Vershbow) 'Build common security, Vershbow urges Russia, NATO', *Johnson's Russia List*, no. 6595, web text, http://www.cdi.org/russia/johnson/6595-9.cfm.

71 V. Baranovsky, 'Russia: a part of Europe or apart from Europe?', *International Affairs*, 2000, vol. 76, no. 3, p. 456.

72 Press Conference by NATO Secretary General, Lord Robertson following the meeting of the NATO–Russia Council. For background on TMD co-operation up to early 2003, see R. Bell, 'Ballistic missile threats: A NATO–Russia strategic challenge', *Krasnaya Zvezda*, 27 February 2003, web text, http://www.nato.int/docu/articles/2003/a030227a.htm.

73 See, *inter alia*, 'First ever NATO–Russia missile defence exercise', web text, http://www.nato.int/docu/update/2004/03-march/e0308a.htm; W. Boese, 'NATO, Russia hold joint missile defense exercise', *Arms Control Today*, 2004, web text, http://www.armscontrol.org/act/2004_04/MDExercise.

74 Keynote Address by NATO Secretary-General, Jaap de Hoop Scheffer, at the NATO–Russia Council Conference on the role of the military in combating terrorism, web text, http://www.nato.int/docu/speech/2004/s040405a.htm.

75 Text available from IISS, London. See also S. Ivanov, 'As NATO grows, so do Russia's worries', *New York Times*, 7 April 2004, web text, http://www.nytimes.com/2004/04/07/opinion.

76 This term, and characterisation of the relationship up to the formation of the NRC, is taken from the author's earlier work: M. A. Smith, 'A bumpy road to an unknown destination? NATO–Russia relations, 1991–2002', *European Security*, 2002, vol. 11, no. 4, pp. 59–77.

77 See, *inter alia, Izvestia*, 30 March 2004. *CDPSP*, 2004, vol. 56, no. 13, p. 22; S. Myers, 'As NATO finally arrives on its border, Russia grumbles', *New York Times*, 3 April 2004, web text, http://www.nytimes.com/2004/04/03/international/europe; J. Page, 'Expanded Nato turns cold war into cold peace', *The Times*, 13 April 2004.

78 J. Steele, 'Transcript of first part of President Putin's meeting at Novo Ogarevo on Monday September 6 2004 with a group of foreign academics and journalists', *Johnson's Russia List*, no. 8369, web text, http://www.cdi.org/russia/johnson/8369-putin.cfm.

6 Russia–NATO relations: what kind of partnership?

1 V. Inozemtsev, 'The US, EU and Russia in the 21st century', *International Affairs* (Moscow), 2002, vol. 48, no. 6, pp. 134–5.

2 T. Hopf, 'Why the United States should cede its Russia policy to Europe' (PONARS Policy Memo 170), web text, http://www.csis.org/ruseura/ponars/policymemos/pm_0170.pdf.

3 A. Stent and L. Shevtsova, 'America, Russia and Europe: a realignment?', *Survival*, 2002–03, vol. 44, no. 4, pp. 121–34.

4 R. Legvold, 'Russia's unformed foreign policy', *Foreign Affairs*, 2001, vol. 80, no. 5, p. 69. See also D. Lynch, *Russia Faces Europe* (Chaillot Paper 60), Paris, EU Institute for Security Studies, 2003, p. 8.

5 *Izvestia*, 1 February 2002. *CDPSP*, 2002, vol. 54, no. 5, pp. 3–4.

6 M. Smith, *Euroatlantic Links: Russian Views*, Camberley, CSRC, 1997, p. 2.

7 M. Smith, *Russian Foreign Policy towards the Far Abroad*, Camberley, CSRC, 1997, p. 7.

8 See S. Talbott, *The Russia Hand: A Memoir of Presidential Diplomacy*, New York, Random House, 2002, pp. 308, 316–17.

9 B. Lo, 'The securitization of Russian foreign policy under Putin', in G. Gorodetsky (ed.) *Russia between East and West*, London, Frank Cass, 2003, pp. 16–17.

10 M. Light *et al.*, 'Russia and the dual expansion of Europe', in Gorodetsky (ed.) *Russia between East and West*, p. 71.

11 V. Baranovsky, 'Russia: a part of Europe or apart from Europe?', *International Affairs*, 2000, vol. 76, no. 3, p. 454.

12 Talbott, *The Russia Hand*, p. 328.

13 Russian Ministry of Foreign Affairs, *Daily News Bulletin (2448–29–10–2003)*, web text, http://www.ln.mid.ru.

14 N. Narochnitskaia, ' "Old" Europe and "new" Europe', *International Affairs* (Moscow), 2003, vol. 49, no. 3, p. 110.

15 *Vremya Novostei*, 13 February 2003. *CDPSP*, 2003, vol. 55, no. 6, p. 2.

16 See, *inter alia*, 'As she did 300 years ago, Russia is turning once again to Europe', *Independent*, 15 May 2003; A. Aslund, 'A Russia resurgent', *New York Times*, 28 May 2003. It should be noted that other commentators argued that the Russian stance had not seriously antagonised the Bush administration mainly because the latter did not 'really believe Russia matters'. Y. Albats, 'When good friends make bad diplomacy', *New York Times*, 28 May 2003.

17 'President Putin, a rigged election and a land ripped apart by civil war', *Independent*, 7 October 2003.

18 See the official American transcript of the summit press conference, 'President Bush meets with Russian President Putin at Camp David', web text, http://www.whitehouse.gov/news/releases/2003/09. For useful analysis of the state of relations, and a desire to mend fences as early as June 2003, see J. Steele, 'From Russia with love', *Guardian*, 5 June 2003.

19 Lynch, *Russia Faces Europe*, p. 14.

20 On the concept of bandwagoning see S. Walt, *The Origins of Alliances*, Ithaca, Cornell University Press, 1987.

21 Smith, *Russian Foreign Policy towards the Far Abroad*, p. 3.

22 V. Israelyan, 'Russia at the crossroads: don't tease a wounded bear', *Washington Quarterly*, 1998, vol. 21, no. 1, p. 50.

23 'Does Russia need NATO, and if so, what kind of NATO?', web text, http://www.nato.int/docu/speech/2003/s031030a.htm.

24 A number of analysts have argued that Russia and the US, in particular, are not natural allies. See, *inter alia*, P. Zelikow, 'Beyond Boris Yeltsin', *Foreign Affairs*, 1994, vol. 73, no. 1, p. 46; M. Bowker, *Russian Foreign Policy and the End of the Cold War*, Aldershot, Dartmouth, 1997, p. 223.

25 For an elaboration of this argument see T. Ambrosio, 'From balancer to ally? Russo-American relations in the wake of 11 September', *Contemporary Security Policy*, 2003, vol. 24, no. 2, pp. 1–28.

26 Aleksei Salmin, quoted in 'Russia's place in the world after September 11', *International Affairs* (Moscow), 2002, vol. 48, no. 2, p. 81.

27 *Vremya MN*, 24 September 2002. *CDPSP*, 2002, vol. 54, no. 39, p. 2.

28 'President Bush Meets with Russian President Putin at Camp David', see note 18.

29 On this see M. Smith, *Russia and Islam*, Camberley, CSRC, 2001.

30 Quoted in *Nezavisimaya Gazeta*, 11 September 2002. *CDPSP*, 2002, vol. 54, no. 37, p. 18.

31 Albeit the term was used only once there. The agreed summit text spoke of 'the potential for building a strategic partnership between the United States of America and the Russian Federation'. See 'A charter for American-Russian partnership and friendship', *Department of State Dispatch*, 1992, vol. 3, no. 25, web text, http://dosfan.lib.uic.edu/ERC/briefing/dispatch/1992/html/Dispatchv3no25.html.

32 V. Kremeniuk, 'Russia and the West: seeking the right distance', *International Affairs* (Moscow), 2000, vol. 46, no. 6, p. 66.

33 Kremeniuk, 'Russia and the West', p. 70.

34 Although some analysts have accorded Russia the status of a *de facto* ally of the US in the wake of the September 11 events. See, *inter alia*, Stent and Shevtsova, 'America, Russia and Europe: a realignment?', p. 123.

35　J. Goldgeier and M. McFaul, *Power and Purpose: US Policy toward Russia after the Cold War*, Washington DC, Brookings, 2003, p. 54. Renée de Nevers has classified US allies in two categories: 'ideological/political' (such as the NATO allies in Europe) and 'strategic', with Russia being in the second group. In effect, however, the notion of a 'strategic ally' amounts to the same thing as the concept of strategic partnership as used here. R. de Nevers, 'Is Russia really an ally?' (PONARS Policy Memo 275), web text, http://www.csis.org/ruseura/ponars/policymemos/pm_0275.pdf.

36　In addition to the US, Russian leaders have also signed agreements describing their relations with China and, more recently, India as being 'strategic partnerships'.

37　A. Kuchins, 'Russia's strategic partnerships and global security' (PONARS Policy Memo 165), web text, http://www.csis.org/ruseura/ponars/policymemos/pm_0165.pdf. On Russia's lack of allies see also Baranovsky, 'Russia: a part of Europe or apart from Europe?', p. 450.

38　A. Lieven, 'The Secret Policemen's Ball: the United States, Russia and the international order after 11 September', *International Affairs*, 2002, vol. 78, no. 2, pp. 245–59.

39　It has certainly had its proponents there, however. See, *inter alia*, A. Iurin, 'Russia and US: partners, no matter what', *International Affairs* (Moscow), 2003, vol. 49, no. 2, p. 41; 'Warm and fuzzy', *The Economist*, 27 September 2003, p. 43; N. Zlobin, 'Nothing is the same anymore', *Johnson's Russia List*, no. 8001, web text, http://www.cdi.org/russia/johnson/8001–12.cfm; N. Zlobin, 'Limited potential, potential limitations: are Russia and the US ready for long-term agreements?', *Johnson's Russia List*, no. 9038, web text, http://www.cdi.org/russia/johnson/9038–9.cfm.

40　'President Putin's Address at the plenary session of ambassadors and permanent representatives of Russia', *Johnson's Russia List*, no. 8290, web text, http://www.cdi.org/russia/johnson/8290–20.cfm.

41　'US-Russian relations: taking relations to a higher level', *Johnson's Russia List*, no. 8163, web text, http://www.cdi.org/russia/johnson/8163–2.cfm.

42　For Robertson's overall assessment of the significance of this and other achievements of the NRC in its first year see 'Does Russia need NATO, and if so, what kind of NATO?'; note 23. For other assessments see *Izvestia*, 1 March 2003. *CDPSP*, 2003, vol. 55, no. 9, pp. 17–18; *Vremya Novostei*, 14 May 2003. *CDPSP*, 2003, vol. 55, no. 19, p. 20; *Vremya Novostei*, 16 June 2003. *CDPSP*, 2003, vol. 55, no. 24, p. 18; Russian Ministry of Foreign Affairs, *Daily News Bulletin (2449–29–10–2003)*, web text, http://www.ln.mid.ru.

43　'NATO, Russian officials praise new spirit of co-operation', *Johnson's Russia List*, no. 7180, web text, http://www.cdi.org/russia/johnson/7180–3.cfm.

44　*Vremya Novostei*, 16 June 2003.

45　'Does Russia need NATO, and if so, what kind of NATO?'

46　For an early hint of possible assistance in Iraq see *Vremya MN*, 11 June 2003. *CDPSP*, 2003, vol. 55, no. 23, p. 18. See also *Rossiiskaya Gazeta*, 21 July 2004. *CDPSP*, 2004, vol. 56, no. 29, p. 18.

47 That is to say, it was placed within the framework of NATO multinational command, control and planning structures.

48 See *Izvestia*, 1 March 2003; *Kommersant*, 24 May 2003. *CDPSP*, 2003, vol. 55, no. 21, p. 17; Russian Ministry of Foreign Affairs, *Daily News Bulletin (2448-29-10-2003)*.

49 Meeting of the NATO–Russia Council at the level of Foreign Ministers held in Istanbul – Chairman's Statement, web text, http://www.nato.int/docu/pr/2004/p040628e.htm.

50 'NATO and Russian ships conduct joint training' (Press Release 37), web text, http://www.afsouth.nato.int/releases/2004releases/PR_37_04.htm.

51 See 'Russian official cautions US on use of Central Asian bases', *New York Times*, 10 October 2003, web text, http://www.nytimes.com; 'Sometimes, two's a crowd', *The Economist*, 30 October 2003, web text, http://www.economist.com.

52 See the text of the treaty, reprinted in *The North Atlantic Treaty Organisation: Facts and Figures*, Brussels, NATO, 1989, p. 376.

53 *Treaty on European Union*, web text, http://www.europa.eu.int/eur-lex/en/treaties/dat/EU_treaty.html.

54 Quoted in 'War in Europe', *The Economist*, 6 July 1991, p. 11.

55 Quoted in N. Malcolm, 'The case against "Europe"', *Foreign Affairs*, 1995, vol. 74, no. 2, p. 68.

56 For a discussion of the respective motivations of the British and French governments in bringing forward the original ESDP proposal, and the relative impact of the Kosovo crisis, see P. Latawski and M. A. Smith, *The Kosovo Crisis and the Evolution of Post-Cold War European Security*, Manchester, Manchester University Press, 2003, ch. 5. The putative ESDP has generated a large academic literature. For a sampling see P. Cornish and G. Edwards, 'Beyond the EU/NATO dichotomy: the beginnings of a European strategic culture', *International Affairs*, 2001, vol. 77, no. 3, pp. 587–603; P. Gordon, 'Their own army?', *Foreign Affairs*, 2000, vol. 79, no. 4, pp. 12–17; F. Heisbourg, 'Europe's strategic ambitions: the limits of ambiguity', *Survival*, 2000, vol. 42, no. 2, pp. 5–15; A. Shepherd, 'Top-down or bottom-up: is security and defence policy in the EU a question of political will or military capability?', *European Security*, 2000, vol. 9, no. 2, pp. 13–30; P. van Ham, 'Europe's common defense policy: implications for the trans-atlantic relationship', *Security Dialogue*, 2000, vol. 31, no. 2, pp. 215–28.

57 'Romano Prodi President of the European Commission: Hearing before the French National Assembly, Paris, 12 March 2003' (Speech/03/126), web text, http://www.europa.eu.int.

58 'Romano Prodi President of the European Commission: "Looking ahead in transatlantic relations" – Washington, 24 June 2003' (Speech/03/322), web text, http://www.europa.eu.int.

59 R. Kagan, *Paradise and Power: America and Europe in the New World Order*, London, Atlantic Books, 2003, p. 3.

60 Kagan, *Paradise and Power*, p. 55.

61 In his March 2003 Paris speech, Prodi said that EU members should not 'exaggerate our differences with the United States . . . we share many views and many chapters of our history. We are trading partners and the great majority of us are military allies of the United States'. See 'Romano Prodi

President of the European Commission: Hearing before the French National Assembly'. Kagan has written that, when the impact of the Iraq crisis subsides, 'the common political culture and the economic ties that bind Americans and Europeans will then come to the fore – until the next international strategic crisis'. Kagan, *Paradise and Power*, p. 96.

62 For a more detailed elaboration of this interpretation of the origins and development of the transatlantic relationship, see Latawski and Smith, *The Kosovo Crisis and the Evolution of Post-Cold War European Security*, ch. 6.

63 See, *inter alia, Kommersant*, 15 May 2002. *CDPSP*, 2002, vol. 54, no. 20, p. 5; *Izvestia*, 29 May 2002. *CDPSP*, vol. 54, no. 22, p. 3; *Konservator*, 13–19 September 2002. *CDPSP*, 2002, vol. 54, no. 36, pp. 16–17; B. Maddox, 'Nato is nowhere and Russia loves it', *The Times*, 8 November 2001.

64 According to Bobo Lo, pragmatism has been 'the nearest thing to a state ideology that exists' in Russian foreign policy in the Putin era. See B. Lo, *Vladimir Putin and the Evolution of Russian Foreign Policy*, London, RIIA, 2003, p. 4.

65 D. Glinski-Vassiliev, 'Suffocation by embrace: The Putin–Bush alliance and the cultural threat to western democracy' (PONARS Policy Memo 226), web text, http://www.csis.org/ruseura/ponars/policymemos/pm_0226.pdf; D. Glinski-Vassiliev, 'The myth of the new détente: The roots of Putin's pro-US policy' (PONARS Policy Memo 239), web text, http://www.csis.org/ruseura/ponars/policymemos/pm_0239.pdf. See also S. Mendelson, 'Wanted: a new US policy on Russia' (PONARS Policy Memo 324), web text, http://www.csis.org/ruseura/ponars/policymemos/pm_0324.pdf.

66 G. Herd and E. Akerman, 'Russian strategic realignment and the post-post-Cold War era?', *Security Dialogue*, 2002, vol. 33, no. 3, p. 370.

67 Goldgeier and McFaul, *Power and Purpose*, ch. 13; Talbott, *The Russia Hand*, p. 404; 'Vladimir Putin's long, hard haul', *The Economist*, 18 May 2002, pp. 25–7.

68 See the transcript of the remarks made by Bush following his meeting with Putin in Slovakia in February 2005. 'President Bush and President Putin discuss strong US-Russian partnership', web text, http://www.whitehouse.gov/news/releases/2005/02/20050224–9.html. See also S. Weisman, 'Powell displays tough US stance toward Russians', *New York Times*, 27 January 2004, web text, http://www.nytimes.com; J. Page, 'Big freeze chills Moscow as Powell voices criticism', *The Times*, 27 January 2004.

69 Lynch, *Russia Faces Europe*, p. 14.

70 The 1995 *Study on NATO Enlargement*, endorsed by the then sixteen NATO members, stated that 'as a general principle, we should avoid new forms of contribution to NATO collective defence which would complicate unnecessarily practical cooperation among Allies and the Alliance's decision-making process'. *Study on NATO Enlargement*, Brussels, NATO, 1995, p. 17.

71 For a thorough overview of the debates in this area see A Kassianova, 'Russia: still open to the West? Evolution of the state identity in the foreign policy and security discourse', *Europe–Asia Studies*, 2001, vol. 53, no. 6,

pp. 821–39. See also, *inter alia*, V. Tolz, 'Forging the nation: national identity and nation building in post-communist Russia', *Europe–Asia Studies*, 1998, vol. 50, no. 6, pp. 993–1022; E. Bajarunas, *Putin's Russia: Whither Multi-Polarity?*, Camberley, CSRC, 2002, p. 7; V. Shlapentokh, 'Is the "Greatness Syndrome" eroding?', *Washington Quarterly*, 2002, vol. 25, no. 1, pp. 131–2.

72 See, *inter alia*, F. Splidsboel-Hansen, 'Explaining Russian endorsement of the CFSP and the ESDP', *Security Dialogue*, 2002, vol. 33, no. 4, pp. 443–56.

73 For a detailed development of this line of argument see I. Straus, 'Western Common Homes and Russian national identities: How far east can the EU and NATO go, and where does that leave Russia?', *European Security*, 2001, vol. 8, no. 4, pp. 1–44.

74 T. Hopf, 'How NATO's war in Yugoslavia is making foreign policy in Moscow' (PONARS Policy Memo 81), web text, http://www.csis.org/ruseura/ponars/policymemos/pm_0081.pdf.

75 C. Wallander, 'US–Russian Relations: between Realism and Reality', *Current History*, 2003, web text, http://csis.org/ruseura/0310_wallander.pdf.

76 For a rare exception see D. Trenin, 'Russia's security integration with America and Europe', in A. Motyl *et al.* (eds) *Russia's Engagement with the West*, London, M. E. Sharpe, 2005, ch. 14.

77 See T. Colton and M. McFaul, 'America's real Russian allies', *Foreign Affairs*, 2001, vol. 80, no. 6, pp. 46–58. Arguably, however, the December 2003 Russian parliamentary election results suggested that, if anything, quite the opposite was happening. See 'Putin's way', *The Economist*, 13 December 2003, pp. 22–4.

78 S. Kortunov, 'Russia's national identity: foreign policy dimension', *International Affairs* (Moscow), 2003, vol. 49, no. 4, p. 100.

Index

eBooks – at www.eBookstore.tandf.co.uk

A library at your fingertips!

eBooks are electronic versions of printed books. You can
store them on your PC/laptop or browse them online.

They have advantages for anyone needing rapid access
to a wide variety of published, copyright information.

eBooks can help your research by enabling you to
bookmark chapters, annotate text and use instant searches
to find specific words or phrases. Several eBook files would
fit on even a small laptop or PDA.

NEW: Save money by eSubscribing: cheap, online access
to any eBook for as long as you need it.

Annual subscription packages

We now offer special low-cost bulk subscriptions to
packages of eBooks in certain subject areas. These are
available to libraries or to individuals.

For more information please contact
webmaster.ebooks@tandf.co.uk

We're continually developing the eBook concept, so
keep up to date by visiting the website.

www.eBookstore.tandf.co.uk